FBI

FIDELITY, BRAVERY,
INTEGRITY

An Autobiography

To good friends
James R. Wright

James R. Wright

iUniverse, Inc.
New York Bloomington

FBI: Fidelity, Bravery, Integrity
An Autobiography

iUniverse books may be ordered through booksellers or by contacting:

iUniverse
1663 Liberty Drive
Bloomington, IN 47403
www.iuniverse.com
1-800-Authors (1-800-288-4677)

Because of the dynamic nature of the Internet, any Web addresses or links contained in this book may have changed since publication and may no longer be valid. The views expressed in this work are solely those of the author and do not necessarily reflect the views of the publisher, and the publisher hereby disclaims any responsibility for them.

ISBN: 978-1-4401-7762-0 (pbk)
ISBN: 978-1-4401-7760-6 (cloth)
ISBN: 978-1-4401-7761-3 (ebook)

Printed in the United States of America

iUniverse rev. date: 10/26/09

CONTENTS

Acknowledgments

I am so grateful to my many friends in the FBI and for their help in writing this book. FBI Agents, Max Noel, LeRoy Teitsworth, Jason Moulton and Tom Healy were all very willing to share their memories and details of the cases. Kay Williams at the Prepublication office of the FBI was very kind and helpful in giving approval from the FBI to write this book. Valerie Holladay from Brigham Young University did a lot of organizing and proof reading. Cody Clark proof read the manuscript, and Melissa Mcoy was a great help with the pictures. My heartfelt thanks to all.

However, I never could have written this book without the help of my wife, Sharon. She has spent countless hours typing the manuscript by listening to my "charming" voice from a cassette tape. She has also helped me remember details of cases by asking questions, suggestions with some of the verbage used, and for the months of love and encouragement. It is nice to have a wife who truly loves you.

FORWARD

Throughout my career as an FBI Agent, it has been apparent to me that the Federal Bureau of Investigation is an elite organization that creates a brotherhood of men and women fighting, often times behind the scenes, to protect the freedoms of our country and fellow Americans. We are often in dangerous situations that require complete trust and confidence in those with whom we work. It really starts with our training. As we learn the methodology of investigating and develop the art of marksmanship, it is always alongside those persons willing to put their lives on the line. We have to depend on each other for help whether it be pulling out our guns to protect one another or throwing out ideas to solve cases. Over the years I have worked with many great men and women. A bond of friendship has been created that will never be broken. Even after retirement, keeping in touch with old partners and associates has been a source of great joy for me.

Chapter One

Modern-day Huck Finn

Writing about one's life can often be tedious, but it is also a great source of joy as memories appear on the written page. I was born September 29, 1943, in Salem, New Jersey, the third boy in the family. I am surprised that my dear mother didn't call it quits after having three boys. My parents had five sons who lived and then finally had a daughter, Elizabeth Elin. Half of us boys feel that we owe our very existence to the fact that my parents kept trying to have a daughter. When I was a year old, my parents moved to Woodbury, New Jersey and bought their first home at 359 South Girard Street, where I lived until I went away to college.

I'm sure my mother didn't have any idea that I would be such a roaming, carefree little boy. Who would have guessed that my life would take me through sports, college, and into the FBI? There were probably some townspeople who thought that Jimmy Wright wouldn't grow up to be worth a plug nickel. But I think that I probably changed their minds through the years as I worked hard to earn money, excelled in sports, and even went on to attend and graduate from college. I hope that they were smiling many years later as they read in the newspapers about my life as an agent in the FBI, working some of the best cases in the Bureau, and about my induction into the National Wrestling Hall of Fame as an outstanding American. The Wright boy turned out okay after all.

As a curious child, I was the self-proclaimed Huckleberry Finn of Woodbury, New Jersey. Woodbury was a wonderful place for a boy to live, and I spent my youth loving to fish and hunt. The woods, lakes, and rivers around Woodbury were my Mississippi River. There was one lake three blocks from my home in one direction and another lake one block from my home in another direction. The lakes were full of large- and small-mouth bass, calico bass, sunfish, blue gills, perch, catfish, and carp. In the woods were rabbits, pheasant, and quail.

I loved to fish in those lakes. I remember fishing from the top of a large pipe that separated two lakes. I caught a lot of fish, and I'd give them to the fishermen there, who would take them home to eat. One day I caught a giant carp. I ran up the street and a neighbor took my picture with the carp. For a young man, that was quite a thrill.

I never got into serious trouble, but I am sure that my mother was sometimes exasperated with me because I was constantly bringing home rabbits, fish, pheasants, quail, and muskrats—dead, of course.

My companion was my dog, Golly, and occasionally my friends or my brother Jeff were involved in my adventures. Golly was a great hunting dog, brown and white and part beagle. I don't have a clue what the other parts were, but he sure was fast for having such short legs. He would always chase out rabbits so that I could shoot them. One time I shot a quail that landed in a lake and I remember Golly jumping into the lake, swimming out, getting the quail, and bringing it back to me.

One day while I was hunting, I saw a rabbit running through an asparagus field and heard Golly barking. I shot several feet in front of where I thought Golly was and immediately he stopped barking. I thought for sure that I had killed him, so I dropped my gun and ran in his direction. Golly was looking down at the dead rabbit. I certainly learned from that experience, and would never again shoot what I could not see.

I was very fortunate to have good parents, Joseph Humphries Wright and Elinor Louise Wright. They stayed married to each other all their adult lives. My father was a very good man, but scraped by most of his life because he did not have a lot of money. He worked hard, though, and always had a job. I remember one Christmas when all of the boys in our family received a bicycle. I will never know how our parents could afford to give each of us a bike. What a wonderful Christmas that was.

I was baptized a member of The Church of Jesus Christ of Latter-day Saints at eight years of age. My family used to attend church in Camden, New Jersey, and the only baptismal font was in Philadelphia, Pennsylvania, so I was baptized in Philadelphia. It was a thrill for me to walk over the Benjamin Franklin Bridge between Camden and Philadelphia.

We got our share of snow and cold winter weather in Woodbury. I used to go sledding, and I would go ice-skating on the lakes near our home. Once in a while, when the ice would cave in, I would fall in water up to my neck. By the time I got home, I would be a walking icicle. It's a wonder that I lived through those years.

Each summer my aunt and uncle, Margaret and Walter Wright, invited my brother and I to stay with them for a week in Cape May, New Jersey. We loved our time in Cape May, fishing, swimming, and just having fun. One day my cousin Walt and I went down to the boardwalk, which was full of amusements. It was built with boards that had spaces between them. When people would pull out their money they would often drop some between the spaces in the boards. Walt and I would go under the boardwalk, sift through the sand, and find a lot of lost coins there. It was fun finding them and having spending money in our pockets.

When I was around eight or nine years old, I joined a little league team and found out that sports came very easy for me. Between ages nine and twelve, I was on a little league team called the Lions. I had good coaches and I loved the sport of baseball. My two main positions were shortstop and pitcher. Over the years I received several awards in baseball, but the one I was most proud of was the highest batting average in little league, at age twelve.

LITTLE LEAGUE

In March of 1962, a severe winter storm hit Cape May and many houses were under water. In fact, my grandmother had to be taken from her home in a rowboat. My uncle Walter was the mayor of Cape May at the time, and he was blamed for not erecting some kind of barrier to protect the citizens of Cape May. My brother Jeff and I hitchhiked down to Cape May after the storm and saw cash registers and many personal items on the beach. That was when Uncle Walter found out that it wasn't fun to be mayor of a city that had just flooded. He used to joke about the flood, telling how he saw a man in a rowboat paddling after his home yelling, "For sale! For sale!"

In the fall, my mother often sat on a chair underneath an apple tree in our back yard, peeling apples. One day I went out to her and noticed that she had dozens of bees walking up and down her arms and hands while she was peeling the apples. I told her she was going to get stung and she replied, "If you don't bother the bees, they won't bother you."

Well, apparently I didn't learn from that because a few days later Golly and I went down to the lake where a very large tree had fallen near the shore. I could hear a buzzing noise inside the tree. Since I sometimes foolishly played with firecrackers and cherry bombs, I decided to drop a cherry bomb down inside the tree. After a very loud explosion, hundreds of bees came out of that tree and began chasing Golly and me down the street stinging us. By the time I got home, I had a couple of bee stings. Bees were coming out of my clothes as I took them off. Clearly I should have paid attention to my mother's advice about not bothering the bees, and they wouldn't have bothered me. It is a wonder that Golly still liked me after that experience. A good dog really is man's best friend. A dog's devotion is unconditional.

Another time when I was out in the backyard, I picked up a wooden basket and found a huge rat underneath. I quickly put the basket back on top of it and yelled to my mother that I had a rat underneath the basket. She said that I probably had a bird. I told her that I knew what rats looked like. She took a wooden stump and whacked it several times. When I lifted the basket again, the rat was dead. I don't think my mother was afraid of anything. And her bravery was certainly a good thing, having five boys to contend with day in and day out.

Because it was extremely humid in the summertime, it was difficult to sleep at night. I asked my parents if I could sleep in the basement where it was cooler. To fully comprehend how desperate I was to sleep at night, it's important to understand what my parents' basement was like. I used to trap rats in our home for my parents. Since my family had chickens, rats would often come into the house. My father paid me twenty-five cents for every rat I killed. I remember one time I heard the trap go off at the top of the stairs to the basement. I saw the rat hobbling down the stairs after getting out of the trap. It was obvious that it was hurt, so I ran after it with a shovel and whacked it several times until it was dead. You can't let twenty-five cents escape! Rats and all, I still wanted to sleep in the basement.

Our family never had much money, so money became very important to me. I remember getting a paper route for the *Courier Post* before I was really old enough to have one. I built up that route until I had over a hundred customers. The Camden *Courier Post* treated their carriers very well, and I won many prizes, including a bicycle, for signing up customers. I also worked hard pulling weeds, shoveling snow, selling Christmas candy, trapping muskrats for their pelts, driving an ice cream truck, painting houses, and working for an electric company. It's amazing the things I would do in order to have spending money.

CHAPTER TWO

School, Sports, and More

Connie Mack Stadium

When I was a child, the Philadelphia Phillies baseball team played in a stadium in Philadelphia called Connie Mack Stadium. My father and I both loved sports, especially baseball. What a great day it would be, a boy and his dad going to a baseball game together. We would often go to the stadium, arriving while the players were taking batting practice. We soon found out that that if we stationed ourselves in the right field bleachers' lower section, lefthanders would often hit foul balls in our direction, and we were sometimes able to get those foul balls.

Connie Mack Stadium was built in the heart of the Philadelphia slums. There was no parking and you had to leave your car on the street. Often young street-wise boys would come up and say, "Sir, if you will give me some money, I will watch your car and make sure that no one will vandalize it." And if you didn't give them money, there was a good chance that your car would be vandalized. You wondered who actually did the vandalizing.

One time while we were waiting outside the stadium, a player hit a home run and it landed on the porch of a house. Several of us boys rushed up to get the ball. I grabbed it and some of the boys jumped on my back. After they got off my back, I jumped up and held up my hand for my father to see I still had the baseball. I knew that he would be proud of me.

Another time I went to Connie Mack Stadium and was able to get two baseballs in one game. My father, however, was the champion. He actually got three baseballs in one game. The front row seats were right next to the field and you could reach down and pick up baseballs inside the fence. One day my father and one of the players got to the baseball at the same time. They wrestled back and forth and my father won. The ballplayer promised my father that if he would let him have the ball he would give it back when they finished warming up. I was surprised to see my father give him the ball, and when they finished, the player did, in fact, give back the baseball. Between my father and me, we really had quite a collection of baseballs, each with a special story to tell.

We were able to go to the last game in Connie Mack Stadium before it was torn down. After the game, people started tearing the place apart to take home pieces of the stadium as souvenirs. People were taking toilets out of the bathrooms, tearing walls out, and even tearing up the field. While we were still in our seats, a man came up to us and asked us if we wanted the seats that we were sitting in. He had a wrench and said that he was taking the seats apart for people who wanted them. My father said that he did want the seats, and we took home two seats from Connie Mack Stadium. Just imagine having a piece of baseball history right in our home to relive the wonderful memories about me, my dad, and the Philadelphia Phillies.

In 1957, I was in the seventh grade. During this time I learned to jitterbug, and I loved to dance. Everyone I knew loved to do the jitterbug. Our school held a dance contest and, of course, the jitterbug was the dance to do. My partner and I won this contest and were each given a case of Coke soda. Inasmuch as I didn't drink Coke, I gave my case of soda to the runner-up. It sure was a lot of fun dancing back then and I still enjoy dancing today with my wife.

Mr. William Morro encouraged me to try out for wrestling when I was a seventh grader at Woodbury Junior High School, and thus began a lifelong relationship with my friend and future wrestling coach. Sports came easily to me and I always had a strong desire to succeed.

In the eighth grade, I had a history teacher who called my name while taking attendance on the first day of class. When I said here, she asked me if I was the brother of another Wright and I told her I was. After that she said to me in front of the whole class, "I will be watching you closely." I guess my older brother had been a bit mischievous when he was in her class.

But I never did have problems in junior high or high school, because I had good teachers and I really wanted to learn. I was always on the honor roll, which meant I got all As and Bs. While in high school, I was on the student council, received the American Legion Award, and was an alternate to Boy's State—a summer leadership and citizenship program sponsored by the American Legion.

For two summers in 1960 and 1961, I worked at Camp Viking in Orleans, Massachusetts, as part of the galley crew. I loved this position and during our off times we were able to fish and sail and do the things the campers did. The campers were children of movie stars and rich people, and had plenty of money. One of the young men with whom I worked with in the galley was named Gerry Drinkwater. Gerry has always been a good friend of mine. He carved tikis, put rawhide straps around them, and then sold them to those rich little kids. Gerry was doing very well and he came up to me and said, "Look, Jim, we can make a lot of money selling these tikis to the campers. Why don't you help me carve them." Gerry gave me a block of wood and a razor and I began to carve. It wasn't long before I realized that I would never be able to carve anything that anyone would want to have. Gerry also realized that I was not a carver of tikis. So he said, "Jim, why don't you do the selling for me and I will carve the tikis." That was when I learned that artwork was not my favorite subject.

I was always thinking up ways to earn that green stuff. In 1960, I went into business with a young man named Kenny Anderson. Kenny and I made a business trapping muskrats and then selling the pelts. It was a fun way to make a living, and Kenny and I were very good at what we did. But those muskrats sure were mean, feisty critters. We would trap and drown the muskrats and then take them to the basement at my home and pelt them. Later we found an individual who would pay us for the muskrats without us pelting them. At the time, we were paid around three dollars for each muskrat, and we trapped lots of them. But it didn't seem to affect the muskrat population too much.

We used two types of traps. In one the muskrat would go into the box trap and couldn't get out, and then would drown when the water got higher. The other trap worked like a bear trap. I was very disappointed one day to find only the leg of an albino muskrat in a trap. Albino muskrats were worth a lot more money than the black or brown muskrats. The muskrat must have felt it was better to lose a leg than to lose its life.

Woodbury High School was very competitive in sports. During my senior year, the quarterback on the football team and I were the only students to receive three varsity letters in three different sports. We were each presented with a sweater during the trophy presentations. I was the number three player in tennis my sophomore year and went undefeated. During my junior and senior years, I was the number one player and captain of the team. I received several medals in wrestling, and as a senior, was second best in my weight class in the state. In cross-country, I was the second-fastest runner in the school. I was not very tall in high school. When I ran races I would look for somebody taller than me and would run to get ahead of him. That helped me a great deal during cross-country. Altogether, I earned seven varsity letters in three different sports

Wrestling Scholarship

I was close to the former athletic director at Woodbury High School, William Morro. He always seemed to take notice of me. He was the varsity wrestling coach, and during my senior year he came up to me and asked where I was going to college. I told him that my family and I did not have any money and I would not be going to college. Mr. Morro responded by telling me that he could get me a wrestling scholarship if I wanted to go to college and also suggested that I go to Annapolis. He said that he was turning in my paperwork to Annapolis in order for me to go. I was grateful to him for this, but I received a reply from Annapolis that I was not accepted because I did not get a sponsor. I didn't know students needed to get a sponsor to go to Annapolis. When Bill Morro asked me why I didn't get a sponsor, I told him that I hadn't been told to get one.

Bill Morro didn't give up there. He told me again that he could get me a wrestling scholarship, and asked me if there was a college that I desired to attend. I told him that I had a couple of friends who were attending Brigham Young University in Provo, Utah. Within a few days, he had secured for me a wrestling scholarship to Brigham

Young University. By the time I graduated from high school, I also had a scholar/athletic award.

I will always be grateful to Bill Morro for his help. I know that I would not have been able to accomplish what I did without his help and guidance.

Bill Morro was more than a good wrestling coach. He was a good friend to his wrestlers. He really cared about what you did with your life. If I had not gone to college with Morro's recommendations, I would never have taught school, coached high school athletes, or had a career with the FBI. That wrestling scholarship opened up many opportunities.

Morro wrote this recommendation for me:

"Wright was an amazing athlete who could succeed at whatever he tried and just needed the chance to explore his abilities. Wright was in the seventh grade when he was playing sandlot ball on the playgrounds in the city. He was about ninety pounds, but he had good hands and all the talent. When he came here, he wrestled but he also ran cross-country and played tennis, and he was good at all three."

My high school graduating class was very large. During my senior year in 1962, our class took a trip to Washington DC, staying in apartments there. We had our picture taken in front of the capitol building with the entire senior class, our principal, and various teachers. Jack, another senior, and I decided that we would run from one side to the other while the picture was being taken. At the time, the photographer would move his camera gradually from the left side to the right side until the whole picture was taken. And so Jack and I were able to be in both sides of the picture.

An interesting side note: I took second in state in wrestling that year, and the heavyweight from our school, John Brennan, took third in state. John was standing about halfway in the middle of the last row and tried to trip me as I ran past. As a result, John's face is blurred and the person next to him is laughing while Jack and I have clear shots on both sides of our class. After we received the pictures, I told John that it was funny I was in it twice and you could hardly tell who he was. The principal was not too happy with our stunt, but he didn't send us home.

I have my graduation picture hanging in my den in Utah. It's interesting how much longer the dresses were in April of 1962.

After graduation from high school, I spent the summer painting houses in order to earn money to help with my college expenses. That was as close to being an "artist" as I would ever get. Through this experience, I became a pretty good painter and it later helped when I owned a home and was able to paint it myself.

CHAPTER THREE

Brigham Young University

Wrestling at BYU

I traveled to Brigham Young University (BYU) with my older brother, David, and two girls from Philadelphia, all of us students there. We traveled nonstop and arrived in two-and-a-half days. Dave and I took turns sleeping and driving. Once we arrived in Provo, Utah, we dropped off the girls and Dave and I looked for an apartment. We found one several blocks from campus, put our money down, and unpacked our suitcases. I loved Brigham Young University from the moment that I stepped on campus. It was beautiful and there were beautiful girls everywhere you looked. I'm not sure which I liked better, the campus or the girls. At the time there were approximately twenty-five thousand full-time students.

I never did have much money while attending BYU. I worked three different custodial jobs on campus for which I was paid one dollar an hour. Today one dollar an hour seems like a terrible wage, but I was glad to have the money back then.

I worked hard as a student, getting good grades and loving the classes I was taking. Since I was at BYU on a wrestling scholarship, I found out where the wrestling room was and began wrestling almost immediately. One of the classes I took the first semester was intermediate wrestling. The first day of class, the wrestling coach came into the room and told the professor that I was on the wrestling team and should receive an A grade, but that I should never have to come to class because I was wrestling a couple of hours each day.

Until then, BYU had never won the Western Athletic Conference in wrestling, and it was my goal to change that. There were five wrestlers in my weight class, the lightest in college wrestling. Three of the young men I could easily defeat. There was another wrestler, however, from California, who initially gave me a hard time. Each time I wrestled with him, he would pick me up and slam me to the mat. He wouldn't drop his knee to the mat first, which was the rule. I would go home from practice black and blue and sore, wondering whether I would ever make varsity.

Two of the best wrestlers on the BYU wrestling team were Mike Young and Mac Motokawa. One day at practice, Mike got on one side of me and Mac got on the other side. They told me that if I wanted to wrestle varsity, then I would have to learn how to leg wrestle. I had never leg wrestled before, but I started "leg riding" so I could learn what to do in order to beat the kid from California. After leg riding for a few weeks, I became very comfortable with it and challenged my California opponent. I beat him for the first time and never lost to him again. Whenever he would challenge me for a position on the varsity team, I would beat him by throwing my legs around him. He never figured out how to escape.

During my freshman year (1962—1963), we had a great bunch of wrestlers, and the campus paper, the *Daily Universe,* always had great articles about the team, for which I was grateful. All of us on the varsity team were freshmen except for the heavyweight, who was a senior. It didn't seem difficult then, but looking back on it, the practices were rough. We would run the stadium steps and I would end up in the steam room with a rubber suit on to lose weight. I always made my weight. Once during the season, I broke my little finger and had to go to the campus infirmary. Coincidentally, a few minutes after I went to the infirmary, Mike Young came in with his little finger broken.

The Western Athletic Conference tournament that season was held in Phoenix, Arizona. Our team rode a bus to the airport in a blizzard and wondered if we would even make it to Salt Lake City. I had never been on an airplane before, but once I was in the plane and we took off, I felt much safer in the airplane than I had driving the forty-five miles from Provo to Salt Lake City in a snowstorm. When we arrived in Phoenix, we went to our hotel rooms and I found out that actors Bob Cummings and Art Linkletter were staying in the same hotel. I was able to get Art Linkletter to write a note to my sister, which I sent to her back in Woodbury.

During my first match, I lost by one point to an opponent when he reversed me with one second left on the clock. I then had to wrestle the captain of the University of Utah team, Ray Campos. I remember that the coach met with us and said that, in order to win the conference title, all of the BYU wrestlers in the semifinals and finals had to win their matches. It was amazing that each of us won our matches, winning the Western Athletic Conference title for the first time in school history.

BYU WRESTLING TEAM

After the matches were over, one of the University of Utah wrestlers came up to me and said, "Jim, come up to my room, I want to show you something." When I got to the room, it was full of women. The bathtub was full of booze, and everyone was drinking. He did this, of course, to embarrass me. I told him that I would not join him and left.

The coach from Brigham Young University was delighted to win the conference and felt sure he could probably win it again the next year, since he would only be losing one person from the entire team. When he realized, however, that half of the members of the varsity team would be leaving for missions for The Church of Jesus Christ of Latter-day Saints, not returning to BYU for two years, he quit his job.

Bob Piper Accident

After the first semester in 1962, my brother left school and another wrestler moved into our apartment with me. His name was Bob Piper. Bob wrestled in the weight class above mine. After the second semester in 1963, when the wrestling season ended, Bob decided that he wanted to go to southern California to see family and friends. At the time, Bob was dating Sue Breton, who was from Philadelphia.

Later, I received a telephone call from Bob's brother telling me that there had been a terrible accident and that both Bob and Sue were in the hospital, unconscious. I decided to travel down to see them and to see if there was anything that I could do to help. Since I didn't have an automobile, the only way that I could get to southern California was to hitchhike. Back in the sixties, it was much safer to hitchhike than it is today.

A couple of different people picked me up. Each time I got dropped off, I would put out my thumb again. One car pulled over and the riders asked me if they could give me a lift. I told them that I would be happy to accept a ride and got into the car. I soon discovered that they were three of the Beach Boys, who were becoming famous at the time with their rock and roll music. The Beach Boys told me that they were tired and asked me if I would mind driving. I told them that it would be fine and I drove the rest of the way to southern California. I certainly didn't realize at the time that I was rubbing shoulders with fame and fortune. However, that was the only time that I would get that opportunity. Fortunately, Bob Piper and Sue Breton eventually regained consciousness and were later able to return to Brigham Young University.

My Future Wife, Karen

I dated a few girls my freshman year at BYU. One girl from California, Lola Jones, told me her roommate, named Karen Sutherland, needed a ride home from Woolworths. Karen worked behind the counter making milkshakes. Although Karen had never met me, I went into Woolworths and said to her, "I'm here to take you home so let's get going."

Karen was startled at my forward suggestion and said, "I don't even know you." Her roommate jumped out from behind the counter, kidding Karen in the process. That was how I met my future wife. So Karen and I started dating, and the more I was with her, the more I fell in love with her.

KAREN AND JIM

Since I didn't have much money, I was delighted to learn that didn't matter to Karen. I would take her down to Skaggs grocery store to buy their special five-cent giant ice cream cone or we would go to twenty-five-cent campus movies.

When I was at Lola and Karen's apartment, I saw that they would light their gas stove in a most unconventional way. They would break off a straw from their broom, light it with the pilot light, and then light the stove. The next day I bought a box of wooden matches and gave them to Karen. It was like I had given her a hundred dollars, she was so happy to get those matches.

After my second semester at Brigham Young University, I returned home for the summer. I hitchhiked across the country to get there. The people picking me up on my trip were kind to me and I really enjoyed the trip. When I got home, my mother was in the side yard with a neighbor. While traveling, I grew a beard and when I approached my mother, she asked, "Can I help you?" not realizing that I was her son. Afterward, I went to the upstairs bedroom where my dog Golly was. When he saw me he started growling and was about to bite me before he finally realized who I was. Golly then became very excited to have me home.

During that summer of 1963, I worked as a truck driver for an electric company owned by Bill Spittle. I really enjoyed the job, hauling large electric wires from site to site. I drove to Nova Scotia to pick up some supplies for Bill. I remember that we rewired the Camden city hall. While I was at the city hall working with an electrician, he took the cables and sliced one of the great big wires in half, not realizing that the electricity was still running in the wire. The entire room filled with sparks and it was amazing that neither he nor I were hurt.

When I returned to BYU in the fall of 1963, I began to work out again as a wrestler and again made the varsity team. It is amazing what you can do when you learn to leg ride. It is as if you have two sets of arms. Just prior to the start of the season, I was leg riding and tore the cartilage in my left leg. I was limping around and could not wrestle. About this time, I went to a campus movie with Karen. While we were waiting in line, another wrestler came up to me and said that I needed to report to the hospital because they were going to operate on my leg. The type of surgery they performed on my leg was the old type of surgery where they sliced you open and cut out the cartilage that was damaged. As a result, I was on crutches for a couple of weeks. I always felt bad that I took Karen to a movie and then couldn't stay to watch it with her.

While recovering, I had to walk on crutches several blocks to campus each day. One time, there was a snowstorm and I had to walk through ice and snow just to get there. Most of the wrestling season came and went while I was recovering. I remember just after I got off the crutches, going to the wrestling room to see how the wrestlers were doing. The California wrestler immediately wanted to challenge me. I told him that I had just gotten off crutches, but he didn't care. So I wrestled him to see which one of us was the better wrestler. And again I was able to defeat him. I realized, however, that my knee was not in good enough shape to wrestle.

I later became heavily involved in various intramural sports: volleyball, swimming, soccer, handball, softball, archery, football, basketball, and others. I loved playing each of the sports and learned a great deal about them.

I majored in history and minored in physical education. The classes I had to take for physical education were interesting. Some of them were kinesiology, physiology of activity, and anatomy. I remember one class where we were working on a cadaver. The girls in the class had no problem grabbing tendons and ligaments, but the boys were a little more timid about handling the cadaver. For a final examination, the professor took us individually to the cadaver and then say something like, "flexor hallucis longus." If the big toe moved when we pulled on the right tendon, we had got the answer correct. I really enjoyed that class.

CHAPTER FOUR

Early Marriage

I proposed to Karen by getting down on my knee and asking her to marry me. I was grateful that she readily accepted. I then went up to Billings, Montana, to meet her parents, Rex and Freda Sutherland. I didn't realize at the time that Rex Sutherland did not like me very much. I later found out that the reason he didn't like me was that Karen was his only daughter. Rex was the head of the music department at Eastern College in Billings, Montana, and I was just a poor kid from New Jersey. Rex Sutherland soon found out that I truly loved his daughter and would do anything for her. As a result, he and Freda became very close to me. In later years, whenever I talked to Rex on the phone he would tell me that he loved me.

Karen and I spent the summer fixing up a home in Springville, Utah. The home had belonged to Karen's uncle, Ray Sutherland, who had passed away. We worked the entire summer on the home, painting it and putting on a new roof.

I married Karen Lee Sutherland in Billings on September 3, 1964. All of my family came from New Jersey to the wedding. Karen's parents went out of their way to make my parents feel comfortable. While we were in Montana getting married, a friend broke into our house in Utah and put Formica on the kitchen counters as a wedding present, which was a nice surprise when we returned to our home.

Fishing at Charleston Bridge

Just prior to the marriage, in the summer of 1964, Karen's father and her brother Lewis came down to Springville to help us put a new roof on the house we were going to live in. One day we decided to take a rest and go fishing at the north end of Deer Creek Reservoir.

We started fishing at Charleston Bridge. As we were walking on the west bank of the river, Rex stepped on a plastic tackle box that was hidden in some bushes. Rather than opening it then to see what it contained, he simply strapped the box to his waist saying he would check it out when he got back to the car. We fished for another hour and a half, until it was dark, then returned to our car. Rex, a college music professor father-in-law-to-be, said, "Let's see what kind of fishing tackle I found," and I grabbed a flashlight. As he opened up the box, it was obvious to each of us that it was full to the top with marijuana. Rex immediately threw the marijuana into the wind. I have never seen anyone as nervous as Rex Sutherland was that night. We've all had a good laugh about this incident since. But just imagine what would have happened if a game warden had stopped us and asked Rex to show him what was in the tackle box that was hanging from his waist.

Prior to getting married, I went to the athletic director at BYU and told him that I needed a good job. He immediately got me a job in the painting and electrical department at Sears, Roebuck in Provo.

On the first day at work, the supervisor of the paint department told me to go upstairs and unload a huge trailer of paint. To show what a keen mind I had, I unloaded the cart of paint from one side, not realizing that the other side would be too heavy with the remaining paint. The cart tipped over and numerous gallons of paint opened up and poured all over the floor. The supervisor walked by me, saw me standing ankle deep in paint, and asked me what was going on. I don't know why he didn't fire me on the spot, and I will always be grateful that he was a patient man and worked with me.

I loved the job at Sears and worked for them for three years. I received several raises during that time, and it was much better than working for a dollar an hour as a custodian on campus.

A man in the shipping department, Garth, became a good friend of mine. One of the things that Garth did at Sears was to go out and repossess items that were not being paid for. Garth was a big strong man. Once he asked me if I would like to go duck hunting with him and I told him that I would. We took his boat to Springville and came to a fenced field where a large bull was roaming. I told Garth that we needed to walk around the field. He said that the bull would not bother us; we could just walk through the field. So we put the boat over our heads and walked to the other side of the field with Garth in front of the boat and me in the back. When we flipped the boat over, the bull was standing about three feet from Garth and about ten feet from me. I was wearing a bright red shirt and the bull took off after me. I was in hip boots and I went over the barbed wire fence without any trouble. Garth also jumped the fence and picked up a two-by-four. As the bull was stamping the ground, Garth took the two-by-four and whacked him on the head. The bull backed off and went the other direction. I will never understand why we weren't arrested for molesting the bull on private property.

I loved being married to Karen, working at Sears, Roebuck, and going to BYU. After working for two years in the paint and electric department, I was transferred to the farm department. While working in the farm department, I was able to take a rototiller home to Springville. At the time, there was a big lot at the back of our yard and I tilled the area, then borrowed a truck and went to my wife's grandmother's farm in Payson, Utah. I filled the back of the truck with chicken manure and brought it back home. I tilled the chicken manure into the soil, and planted one hundred tomato plants and fifty pounds of potatoes. I did not realize how many tomatoes you can get from a hundred tomato plants or how many potatoes fifty pounds actually produced. The potatoes were huge and the tomatoes were coming out everywhere. We couldn't can them fast enough and began giving tomatoes to neighbors. What a great garden we had that year.

Karen's grandmother, Ethel Grace Gardner Hirst, really loved to visit us. Grandma Hirst would chase me around the yard in Springville trying to get a kiss from me. She was quite the driver. I remember one time when I was with Karen, I saw a car whizzing past us and I said to her, "Wasn't that your grandma?" And Karen said, "That was her. She drives very fast."

Hunting

I used to hunt pheasant at Grandma Hirst's farm in Payson. The first time I went down to the farm, Karen's uncle and her cousin were already there at the farm waiting for me. They told me that we needed to walk through the cornfield to the end and when we got to the end, there would be pheasants jumping out of the field. I thought that they were crazy, but I decided to do what they said. When we got to the end of the field, pheasants were flying out of there left and right. I took three shots with my shotgun and knocked down three cock pheasants. The limit for pheasants was three, and it didn't take long to get my limit. I certainly learned a lot about pheasants that day. They are good to eat too.

While walking around the farm, I saw a giant beehive in a tree. The beehive was shaped like a big round circle. I thought that the hive would be a great thing for Karen to use when she was teaching elementary school, so I cut down the limb of the tree and put it in the front seat of my car. Then I went in and visited with relatives for a while. When I came back out, I jumped into my car, not realizing that it was now full of bees. You could certainly tell that I was a city boy. I quickly jumped out of the car and was able to get rid of the bees and still save the beehive for Karen's class.

I used to go deer hunting during the three years that I lived in the Springville home while going to school. The first year I hunted, I borrowed a .30-30 from an uncle, not realizing you needed to sight the gun first. I went to the side of a mountain and sat there and waited for a few minutes before I saw a giant deer on the mountain next to us. So I sighted the deer with my .30-30 and fired at him. The bullet hit about ten yards below the deer. I realized that I had a problem with the gun so I aimed about ten yards above the deer as he was running and he dropped dead on the spot. When I got to the deer, I saw how big mule deer can be. I took him back, skinned and cleaned him, and cut him up for roast, chops, and steaks and we ate deer for a year. The next year, I bought a new .30-30 rifle, lever action Marlin. That rifle was as accurate as can be. Each year I would kill a deer and then we would eat the meat for a whole year. I never went deer hunting without seeing a deer within forty-five minutes to an hour. Back in the 1960s, there were deer everywhere. Many times deer hunters would walk around all day and never see a deer, because deer have great hearing and will not move if someone walks near them. I found out early that if you could get a site where you could see a couple of slopes and just sit there, eventually you would see deer.

Another time I shot a buck on top of a mountain and watched him drop, but when I went over there to slit his throat, I realized the buck had gotten up and run off. My companion and I trailed blood for approximately twenty minutes, following the deer into a wooded area with lots of leaves. That was when I stepped right on the deer. Although this may sound hard to believe, that deer had covered himself with leaves to hide. When I stepped on him, he jumped up and lifted me off the ground. My first shot went straight up into the sky but I managed to compose myself and as the deer was running away, I shot and killed him. I will never forget that experience.

It is amazing what deer can do. I remember seeing an article in a Utah paper about a man who went deer hunting with a brand new .30-06 rifle. The man took a friend with him to take a picture if he shot a deer. He did get a deer with a big rack and then went to slit his throat. As he got close, the deer jumped up and charged him. He couldn't get his rifle in position in time to shoot the deer again, so he just used the rifle to protect himself and the gun got locked in the horns of the deer. Finally, the deer ran off and the friend took a photo of the deer running down the mountain with the rifle in his rack. The man never did find his rifle.

One time Karen and I went fishing in the Provo River. I believe at the time the limit was ten trout each. We were catching fish left and right and putting them into a bag. Karen was about nine months pregnant with our first child. She said that she wasn't feeling well and was going to go up to the car and sit. While she was sitting in the car, I continued catching more trout. A man then came up to me and asked how many trout had I caught. I told him that my wife and I had caught nineteen trout. I caught one more trout and the man said that he was a ranger and asked me to take the trout out of the bag and count them. Fortunately, I had counted correctly and I didn't get into trouble. Incidentally, my wife had our first child the next day.

Cheryl Lee Wright was born July 28, 1966, in Provo, Utah. At the time, Karen's doctor in Springville was Dr. Nance. After Cheryl was delivered, I went to the doctor and asked how Karen was and then asked about the baby. Dr. Nance said that because I asked about Karen first, I would receive a cheaper bill. We don't have doctors like that anymore.

In December of 1966, I traveled with Karen and Cheryl to Billings to celebrate Christmas with Karen's parents. I was driving a four-cylinder Tempest station wagon and we were traveling in a snowstorm. As I approached an intersection, I didn't know whether I should turn left or right so I turned left and immediately realized I had made a mistake. I pushed the clutch pedal down and it went to the floor and would not come back up. I managed to get to a gas station that was close by and learned that we were at least fifty miles from the nearest town.

I went into the gas station with my wife and four-month-old daughter and asked the woman behind the counter if she knew of anyone who could help me. She didn't, but her brother happened to be there and he went out and looked under our car. When he came back, he said, "Your problem is that you lost your clutch rod." He told me that there were some abandoned cars in the back of his sister's gas station and he would try to find a clutch rod that would work.

After cutting the clutch rod out of one of the cars, he realized that it was too long and that he needed to do some metal work. He worked for the state highway department and was able to go to the facility where he worked. He spent a long time cutting the clutch rod and then returned and put the new clutch rod in. When he told me to turn on the engine, it worked perfectly. About this time I was starting to get very nervous, because I didn't have much money at all and I didn't know how much money he was going to charge me. When I asked him how much money I owed him, he just said, "Merry Christmas." That was the nicest Christmas present I ever received.

We then traveled up to Billings, had a wonderful time with the family, traveled back home, and never had problems with the clutch rod again.

When Karen's younger brother Alex was accepted at BYU, he moved in with us in Springville. We enjoyed having him and Alex and I had a good time together playing games. At Christmas, the farm department at Sears became the toy department, and that Christmas, the supervisor of the farm department told me that he had an older and very expensive HO train set that he would sell to me for five dollars. I instantly bought the train set and took it home. It had everything, including boxcars that would explode by shooting missiles at them. Alex and I certainly wasted a lot of time that Christmas with that train set. You are never too old to play with trains.

It wasn't all play, though. From 1965 to 1967, I was the elder's quorum instructor in our Springville ward. I loved the calling, but I never knew why I was called. I didn't know if I was called because I was a good instructor or because they asked several other people who turned them down. Anyway, it helped me a great deal in learning to teach people.

In order to travel between Springville and Provo, I bought a moped. Springville and Provo are approximately five miles apart. To get to Provo, I would ride my moped up a big hill. About halfway up the hill, my legs would get so cold that my ankles would turn numb. I liked it when my ankles would turn numb because the pain would go away. At the time, I could purchase gasoline for twenty-two cents a gallon at an independent gas station owned by Jack Curtis. Isn't it amazing how gas prices have changed?

JIM AND CHERYL ON MOPED BIKE

I worked extra hours at Sears during Karen's senior year so she could graduate. She then helped me graduate by teaching elementary school in Park City, Utah, during my senior year. When I graduated from Brigham Young University, I did not owe money to anyone. My senior year, however, I purchased a brand new 1967 Mustang. It was a great car. The car cost me $2,400.

Car Problems

The following Christmas, we traveled in the Mustang to Billings to celebrate again with Karen's parents. When we started the trip back to Springville, we ran into a terrible blizzard. Cars and trucks were going off the road all over the place. I thought we had made it through successfully, when the right front tire of our Mustang got caught in the snow and pulled us off the road and into a snowdrift. The car was almost completely under the snow. I left my wife and daughter in the car and exited by crawling out a window, looking for a way to get the car out. As I started up the road, I noticed a snowplow coming and I waved down the driver. He pulled our car out of the snow with a chain without any trouble. Surprisingly, there was no damage to the car and it started right up. We traveled the rest of the way home without any problems.

Over the years I put 269,000 miles on that Mustang and finally sold it for $3,000. It was sad to see the new owner drive off in my old Mustang, but it was nice to make a profit after putting so many miles on the car.

1967 FORD MUSTANG

CHAPTER FIVE

Teaching and Coaching

A Step Up to the Future

During my senior year at BYU, I did my student teaching at Springville High School under Phillip Bird, who was an outstanding teacher. I taught history, physical education, and wrestling, and it was a wonderful experience.

When I started looking for employment as a teacher I almost took a position in New York City teaching problem children, but then was offered a job in Centerville, Utah, teaching junior high school kids. Centerville is part of the Davis County School District and, at the time was one of the highest-paying school districts in the state.

While looking for a place to live in Centerville, I found an old torn-up house and decided to play a joke on Karen. I told her I had found a perfect place to live, but that it needed some repairs. I then drove Karen to the house, and as we pulled up in front of it, a large pig walked out of the living room onto the front porch. It was a good thing for me that my wife has a sense of humor.

That same year, I was called to be the priest quorum advisor in my church. At Centerville Junior High, I was assigned to teach history and physical education, which were my major and minor subjects at BYU. I was also assigned to teach geography, which was something I knew nothing about. But I learned to love geography. Four of us teachers team taught with Carl Birmingham as the head teacher. It was really fun working with him and the other teachers, and Centerville was the only school in the district that succeeded in team teaching, which really helped the students.

Even though Centerville was one of the highest-paying school districts, Utah was one of the lowest-paying states. I was paid only $5,000 for my teaching assignment plus $200 for coaching basketball and track.

Centerville Junior High School was a brand new school, and the students were all from a farm area. They were all well-behaved students. I remember one of the students, Mike Belnap, who was a great athlete. While batting in baseball, Mike was hit in the eye with a fast pitch and it put out his eye. In spite of the fact that he only had one eye, he was still the best athlete in the whole school. The only problem he had was that while dribbling the basketball, sometimes he would have the ball stolen from him because he did not have good peripheral vision.

When I coached basketball at Centerville, I knew very little about what was expected, so I trained myself to coach the sport. We had an outstanding team and it was interesting how important basketball was in the junior high schools in Utah. The entire school would come out to the games. The band would be there and there would not be enough room for everyone to sit down. It was so loud at these basketball games that you could hardly hear yourself giving signals. I also helped coach the track team, and we had a very good track team that year. While teaching, I learned the first names of a couple of hundred students. It was a good thing I was young then, because I couldn't do it today.

At the end of the school year, my mother called me from New Jersey and told me that my father had had a heart attack. She said that the heart attack was very hard on him and that he was going through severe depression. My mother knew that my father and I were very close, and she asked me if I could come back to Woodbury for the summer. So Karen, Cheryl, and I jumped into our Mustang and drove back to New Jersey. I soon realized how depressed my father was, and I started doing things with him. He came out of his depression and was making real progress. My mother asked me if I could stay because I was helping my father so much. I had to decide whether to return to the school that I loved in Utah or stay in New Jersey. At the time, the athletic director at Woodbury High School was my friend and former wrestling coach, William Morro. He told me that if I wanted to teach history at Woodbury, he would get me a teaching contract, and that I could coach wrestling. So I decided to accept a position teaching at Woodbury Junior High School, as well as coaching wrestling and freshman baseball at the high school.

I then had to drive back to Centerville to pick up our belongings and to tell the Centerville principal, Paris Curtis, that I would not be returning to teach in the fall. I felt really badly about this, because the principal had treated me so well and had given me everything I had asked for. Principal Curtis seemed to understand, however, and there was no problem.

In September of 1968, I began teaching history at Woodbury Junior High School.

That first day of school, the auditorium was filled with all the students and two boys were punching each other. I knew one boy was the son of the principal, Russ Hawk, and the other boy was the son of the geography teacher. I called them both out of the auditorium and stood in the hall talking to them. The principal saw me take them out and quickly followed. He asked me what the problem was and I told him that these two young men did not know how to behave themselves. At that time I really did not know Russ Hawk, but I was anxious to know if he was going to back me or back the students. Russ Hawk took the two young men, pushed them against the wall, and then marched them down to his office with me. He was so hard on those students that I felt sorry that I had taken them out of the auditorium. However, those two young men became the best-behaved students I had during my first year of teaching. I enjoyed my experience at Woodbury Junior High School very much, and I really enjoyed working with the teachers and the principal.

One day while teaching, a student in the back of the class was making noises like an animal. I told him to stop and he continued, so I took him out into the hall and pushed my finger into his chest. He hit the wall behind him. Later that day, the student brought his father in, who demanded to know what was wrong with his son. I met with him, the student, and the principal in the principal's office. I told the father that his son kept making noises like an animal and the father almost whacked his son in front of us. From that point on, the student knew how to behave himself.

In those days, teaching was an enjoyable experience because you had the backing of the students' parents. It is a lot harder today.

Although the high school did have some problems with white and black students having fistfights, the junior high school did not. On a few occasions, the local police were called in to stop fights in the high school. My younger brother Jeff was a police officer in Woodbury and was one of the officers called to step in.

My first year, I coached freshman baseball. It was such a fun experience, teaching a sport that I knew well. Our team was undefeated and the varsity coach kept calling on freshmen to move up to varsity because they were so good. It was easy to coach those kids. I could call any play and the team would always get it because they were such good athletes.

I was also the head varsity coach for the high school wrestling team, but our team was only average and we lost more matches than we won. This was very disappointing to me because I knew so much about wrestling, and I felt that I taught them a lot. So I set up an intramural wrestling program for junior high school students. I talked several students into participating, including Howard Pendleton, who later became a state champion in wrestling. It is amazing how you can be undefeated in one sport and average in another sport. I also taught two years as the varsity tennis coach. We had a great tennis team although I didn't feel as though I taught them as much as I taught my less successful wrestling team.

I had to do many things to stay ahead financially as a teacher. I supervised a summer painting crew. I taught history on the side to handicapped students. I also taught history to pregnant high school girls so they would be able to graduate. When a girl became pregnant, she would have to leave school, but nothing would happen to the boy who got her pregnant, which I thought was very unfair.

On Saturday mornings, I taught a law enforcement class to gifted seniors at Woodbury High School. I took the students to court sessions and had the mayor, police officers, and others come to speak to them. It really was a fun class to teach.

While I was teaching and coaching, I was called to be president of the young men in my church to work with the youth aged twelve to eighteen. My calling involved teaching and planning activities for them. It certainly kept me busy. My sister Elin, was in the same age group as the young men, and participated in some of the activities. I remember making hoagie sandwiches in my garage to sell in order to make money for the young adults. The youth would take the sandwiches to their neighborhoods to sell, and all the profits would go to them. There were so many people who wanted sandwiches that we couldn't make enough. Once there was a terrible car accident on the New Jersey Turnpike near my home. We sold hoagies to the people who were in the accident.

One evening, I went to a dance and opened up a closet door to find a couple making out on the floor. I also remember dancing with my sister Elin, who was a high school student. She loved to borrow my 1967 Mustang. Mustangs were very popular with teenagers. It was a great experience for my sister, who talks about my Mustang even today.

When I first began teaching at Woodbury Junior High School, Karen and I rented an apartment for one year at the Woodbury Terrace apartments. Karen taught half-day kindergarten and we used the money she made to make the down payment on the home we purchased in Woodbury Heights for $16,000. My uncle Walter, who was an attorney, did the paperwork for us, and we were able to buy and move into our first home.

Since Karen and I were both teaching, we needed a babysitter for Cheryl for a half day. I asked my mother if she would take care of Cheryl, and she said certainly. But when I told her how much I would pay her, she told me that she would not accept any money. I told her that she could not babysit if she did not take the money. So she agreed.

That entire summer, my mother saved the money I gave her in a jar. My mother came to our house to help us pack for a visit to Billings. After we arrived in Billings, we unpacked our suitcases and discovered the money that we had given to my mother. She had put it in our suitcase without us knowing it. It felt nice to have a mother who really cared about us.

While in Billings, we left Cheryl with Karen's parents and we went up the mountain with a .22 pistol. On top of the mountain, I saw a jackrabbit about 100 yards away. I asked Karen if she would like to shoot at it. She said yes, which was surprising to me. She took one shot and it hit right where the rabbit's feet were. Now can you imagine shooting at a rabbit a hundred yards away with a .22 pistol? I couldn't believe what a good shot she was, and I took the gun back and never asked her to shoot again. It was obvious that she could shoot that pistol better than I could.

On September 23, 1969, our second child, James Aaron, was born at Underwood Memorial Hospital in Woodbury. After his birth, I went to see him at the hospital. Jimmy was a large baby with cauliflower ears, like many large babies have. When I went to see Karen, I told her how beautiful her son was and she replied, "How can you say that when he has those large cauliflower ears?" I hadn't noticed the ears, but I had noticed he was a male.

Jimmy was a blond baby who almost immediately got into trouble. He would stand at the top of the stairs after he learned to walk and pretend that he was jumping off the stairs in order to scare people. He spilled boiling water off the stove onto his head and had to be taken to the hospital. He also had several seizures. But he survived all of his adventures and is healthy today.

CHAPTER SIX

FBI Training

From 1968 to 1971, while I was teaching, my secretary was a woman by the name of Pat Carter. Her husband was a special agent for the Federal Bureau of Investigation. One day Pat said to me, "Jim, why don't you join the FBI? It pays a lot more money and you would love being an agent." At the time, the Bureau was looking to add new agents and wanted to hire one thousand recruits to combat plane hijackings. But I was having so much fun teaching I couldn't imagine having more fun being an agent. Pat told me that if I would apply for the FBI she would even type my application.

Anybody who knows anything about the FBI knows how thorough those applications were and how difficult they were to type. So I agreed to let her do it. After she typed the application, I signed it and sent it in. This was during my third year of teaching. To my surprise, I received a letter from J. Edgar Hoover telling me that I had been accepted as a special agent in the FBI and how much I would be paid.

As I said earlier, Utah pays some of the lowest salaries in the country to teachers and New Jersey pays some of the highest. When I went from Utah to New Jersey, I nearly doubled my salary. I nearly doubled my salary again when I went from teaching school in New Jersey to being a special agent in the FBI. The date that I was assigned to be a special agent in the FBI was June 21, 1971. I was accepted under the FBI's modified program, which is a harder program to be accepted into. Nevertheless, this worked out fine since I could finish teaching at Woodbury before I started as a special agent in the FBI.

When the high school principal heard that I was considering going into the FBI, he called me into his office. I remembered that when I applied for and received a wrestling scholarship to Brigham Young University in 1962, I thought that I might also apply for a scholastic scholarship. When I was a high school student, the principal wrote a letter to Brigham Young University and told them that I was an overachiever. The same principal of the high school, when I was teaching, called me into his office and said that I should not consider the FBI because I was about to get tenure and that I was an excellent teacher. He then asked me why I would consider joining the FBI. I told him that it would nearly double my teaching salary. What could he say to that? I knew about the letter the principal had written to BYU during my senior year of high school, because his secretary was a friend and showed my parents the letter.

Why I Became a Special Agent with the FBI

There are probably four reasons why I became a special agent in the FBI. The first reason, as mentioned already, was that my secretary at the school was married to an FBI agent and told me how great it would be for me to be an agent. The second reason was the increase in salary that I would receive being a special agent. The third reason was that my good friend, Gerry Drinkwater, was a clerk at the FBI office in Philadelphia from 1965 to 1968. Gerry would often tell me how wonderful it was working for the FBI.

The fourth reason, and probably the most important one, was that I read a book about Barbara Mackle, a twenty-year-old who was kidnapped in Florida. Her father, a building contractor, was forced to pay a $500,000 ransom. The book was entitled *Eighty-Three Hours Till Dawn*. Barbara's father, Robert F. Mackle, was a wealthy individual. The agents working the case found out the approximate area where she was being held in a small underground box, essentially being buried alive. The agents found her buried in a plywood and plastic box under the ground in a pine forest in Duluth, Florida. The box was equipped with an air pump, a battery-operated lamp, fan, water laced with sedatives, and food. Barbara Mackle had been buried underground for eighty-three hours when ten agents, crawling on their hands and knees, found the air pipe. They dug her up and pulled her from her would-be grave. You can imagine how she looked after eighty-three hours in the ground. After coming up from her gravesite, she gave each of the agents a hug. There were tears in the agents' eyes by the time she finished hugging them. That story caused me to think about leaving teaching and coaching and joining the FBI.

Background Investigations for the FBI

Agents conducting background investigations for FBI applicants are required to interview supervisors and co-workers, to review personnel records at former employments, to interview references, neighbors, acquaintances, roommates, and to verify college education. It was interesting to learn what questions were being asked of the people I knew as FBI agents conducted my background investigation

For example, question one might be. Did the person know me socially or professionally? Next the agents would ask, What type of character did I have? Was I honest, hardworking, trustworthy, mature, and friendly? What would the people being questioned say about my abilities and the people I associated with? Did they have a good character and reputation? What about my reputation? Had I ever had anything to do with illegal drugs? Had I abused alcohol or prescription drugs? Had I ever been a subject or suspect in any criminal investigation, or had I ever been treated for any emotional problems? Had I ever traveled outside of the United States? And, if I had, were there any foreign counterintelligence issues that needed to be discussed or any unusual or suspicious problems? What about my loyalty, my financial responsibility, my business credit issues? Had I ever had any problems with collection agencies, bankruptcies, and delinquent student loans or had I ever lived beyond my means? Was I prejudiced or biased toward any group of people or individuals? What about my physical condition?

If there were any negative comments, those comments needed to be explored. The agents would then ask the individual being interviewed if he or she was aware of any conduct or activity in my background that could be used in any way to subject me to influence, pressure, coercion, or compromise or that would impact negatively on my character, reputation, judgment, or discretion. Would the individual recommend me for a position of trust and confidence, and in the case of a Special Agent of the FBI, would they recommend me for this position? As these questions show, the investigations are quite detailed and expensive to conduct. The FBI invests a lot of money in checking out their special agents.

People who were accountants or attorneys were given preferential treatment with the FBI. People who spoke certain foreign languages were also hired. There was also a program called the modified program. In the modified program, agents were hired who had graduated from an accredited college and then worked for three years in the area in which they graduated. Inasmuch as I had graduated in teaching and taught school for four years, I was eligible. It is harder to become an agent under the modified program than it is to become an agent with an with an accounting or law background.

FBI Training

The training program for the FBI, back in 1971, was in Washington, DC, as well as at Quantico, Virginia. Agents in training were sent back and forth between the two cities as the FBI Academy in Quantico had not yet been built. The training was for a fourteen-week period and the starting salary for trainees was $11,517 a year. When an agent graduated from his training, he would then be given another $3,000 or more for putting in extra hours. At the time, and still today, agents are required to work fifty hours a week and then were paid another twenty-five percent of their salary when assigned to one of the offices throughout the country. Today, of course, an agent is paid much more money, and if he or she works hard, can be paid up to $100,000 toward the end of his or her career.

The fourteen-week training took place both night and day, and only those agents who lived close enough could go home on weekends. Training for the FBI was quite an extensive program. Agents learned about fingerprinting, criminal law, making arrests, proper procedures for handcuffing, making plaster casts of tire tread marks, shooting various weapons, dropping tear gas into a building, shooting at night, among other skills. I remember that the legal training we took in class was always followed by a test. The trainee needed to make eighty percent on all the examinations; receiving a grade lower than eighty percent on two separate occasions meant the trainee was no longer registered for the class.

The classes in 1971 consisted of fifty trainees in each class. Everyone was required to wear a white shirt. If an agent forgot and wore a colored shirt, he was humiliated by our counselor and never made that mistake again.

We were required to perform various physical activities during training. One time in Washington, we went to the gym and the instructor put two agents in a ring with boxing gloves. The two agents were told that they could do anything they wanted to win this fight, and there were some serious confrontations. The running and physical activities never bothered me, because I was used to working out from my time at BYU.

One of my favorite classes was shooting. During the first day of shooting, the counselor asked the fifty agents in our class who had never shot a .38 revolver. Another agent and I were the only two who raised our hands. The instructor then said, "You two will probably be two of the best shooters, because you didn't pick up any bad habits."

Shooting became one of my favorite things to do, and I learned how to shoot well. At night, however, we had to shoot in the pitch black and load our weapons and shoot at a target that was some distance away, which was very difficult to do. I remember my first attempt. I locked my arm in so that I would fire in the same spot every time. We were supposed to shoot in the K5 area of the target, meaning the "kill zone" parts of the body—the head and torso. After we shot fifty rounds, the lights were turned back on and we pushed the buttons to have our targets brought back to us. I was surprised to find out that there was not a single hole in my target. I had been sure that I was shooting at the same place, but it just was not going into my target. Eventually I learned how to shoot in the dark; I hit my target and I began to enjoy that as well.

There was another shooting place on the range at Quantico called

Hogan's Alley. Many of our youth today know about Hogan's Alley because it's been made into an arcade game. But for special agents at that time, Hogan's Alley consisted of several buildings with a road running down the middle of the town. An agent was required to walk down the street, and as bad people (dummies) jumped out of windows and alleys, the agent was required to shoot them. However, I had to make a judgment as to who were the good people and who were the bad people. I was convinced that I could win this contest. I remember going down Hogan's Alley and shooting all the right targets very quickly. I got right to the end of Hogan's Alley, thinking that I might have won, when a grandmother jumped out of the alley and without thinking I shot her.

There is a tower in Hogan's Alley and in the tower is a shooting counselor. I remember him saying over the loudspeaker, "Way to go, Wright! You just shot a grandmother!"

Another one of the events that we had at training school was a contest to draw and shoot. Two agents would stand next to each other and the counselor would push a button and a metal target would turn to face the agents. Once the button was pushed, the agents were required to draw their weapons and shoot. We heard a ping when we would hit the target. We had fifty agents in the class and it got down to two finalists, another agent and me. We had to be very careful during the draw and shoot contest because if we put a finger in the trigger guard, it would be easy to shoot a hole in our leg. I really wanted to win this contest, but when the last button was pushed, guess who lost? I did.

Just before agents graduated from training, they were required to shake hands with the director of the FBI, who at the time was J. Edgar Hoover. Agents were told they needed to dry their hands so they weren't wet and sweaty, and to look the director directly in the eye as he shook the agent's hand. The inference was that if we did not do those things, we might not be an agent, although this was only a one-time event where the director would officially recognize us as a new agent.

On one occasion, in Washington, I got into an elevator. After I got in the elevator, J. Edgar Hoover and several of his men came in while I stood silently behind them. I didn't want to be in that elevator and I was glad to keep my mouth closed while we rode.

After approximately twelve to thirteen weeks of training, we were told where our first office would be. One by one, each agent was told where he would work for the next year. I was very grateful to be assigned a small office in New Haven, Connecticut. It was a real advantage to work in a small office, because new agents got to work most of the cases the small offices handled.

GRADUATION FROM FBI TRAINING

When I got my orders to go to New Haven, Karen and I put our house up for sale. While I had been training in Washington and in Quantico, Karen had begun painting the inside of our house thinking it would be easier to sell the house if she changed the family room and hallway from blue to a light beige. One day our next-door neighbor came over to visit and brought a friend. The friend asked Karen how much we were selling the house for. She told him $24,000. We had just purchased the house two years before for $16,000. Our neighbor's friend told her that she could stop painting because he was willing to pay that amount and he didn't like the color beige. It made it a lot easier for us knowing that the house was sold, and that we did not have to go through a realtor.

CHAPTER SEVEN

FBI—New Haven, Connecticut

Training in My First Office

In September 1971, I arrived in New Haven, Connecticut, and reported for work. During this time, first office agents were learning to be agents and were considered "green." As a result, first office agents normally did not get really good cases assigned to them. My wife and I liked New Haven and found a place to live in Cheshire. For the next year I served as the stake athletic director in our church. One of the things that I did while in this assignment was to set up a track tournament for the entire stake. It turned out to be a great activity.

But that first week or two in Connecticut, another first office agent and I were assigned to handle telephone duty in the office. Telephone duty normally meant that you answered the phone and tried to answer the caller's questions. We were assigned to work from midnight to 8 AM. in the morning. This got to be a very monotonous assignment. I was amazed to discover how many people are mentally unstable. The

FBI called people who are mentally unstable "51-50s." One night while I was handling the phones a 51-50 called. He was definitely crazy. After talking to him for a few minutes, I received another call and put the first person on hold. The second caller was also clearly a 51-50. Just for fun, I connected the two people and put them over the intercom so that we could listen to their conversation. It lasted most of the evening and it was interesting what two people say to each other when neither is mentally stable. While this incident was amusing, it is unfortunate that many of the 51-50s in this country are too dangerous to be considered amusing.

While I was in New Haven, I was able to work many different kinds of cases—extortion, bank robberies, foreign counterintelligence cases, car ring activities, and organized crime. I even worked a top ten case. This case took us into a ghetto neighborhood late at night, but we were unable to catch the fugitive.

I worked a car ring case run by a man named Lenny Wesnewski. At the time, the FBI got involved in car ring activities because people were stealing cars, cutting them up, and selling the parts. Lenny Wesnewski had such a shop and he was constantly stealing cars and cutting off their serial numbers. When he was arrested, there were a few people in his shop, and a few doors to exit. The FBI surrounded the shop and arrested each of the employees as they were running around trying to find a place to escape.

I also worked a case in West Haven, Connecticut, at a federal hospital. A man entered a patient's room and stole the patient's leather jacket and his wallet with credit cards. An employee saw the man steal the items and chased him through the parking lot, tackling him and holding him for us at the facility. The case went to trial and I had to testify. The person who stole the leather jacket and wallet was black, and he stated during the trial that the only reason he was being charged was because it was a black harassment case. But since the victim and the person who held the thief were also black, it didn't take the jury very long to find this person guilty.

On November 6, 1971, I was one of twenty-five New Haven agents sent to Boston, Massachusetts, for a case involving sports gambling. We kicked in a door to the house, went inside, and found numerous telephones and an individual answering them. There was also a great deal of money there. The person I talked to in the home told me he never would have done it if he thought he was going to get caught. I thought that was an interesting way of looking at it. We hit approximately twenty-five booking places at the same time. It was fun to see all of the money piled up in the Boston office after serving search warrants at each of the booking sites.

In another case, our office received a call from the Boston office about a car ring case. The caller said that agents from Boston were following a stolen vehicle and were heading down to New Haven. Could the New Haven agents "pick up" the car and trail it to find out its final destination? I was one of two units told to follow the car, each unit in his own vehicle. We picked up the trail of the stolen car and the Boston agents were then able to "burn off," and let us take over. We surveilled the car as it traveled toward New York City, and when we thought the car was going to New York City, we had the New Haven office call New York so that they would meet us when we got to a bridge going to New York. We followed the vehicle down to New York, but could not get the New York agents on the air. We then followed the stolen vehicle over the bridge and wound up in the Bronx, where we lost the car.

I realized when we got into the Bronx that I had lived a very sheltered life. In the Bronx, several vehicles were parked and stripped of their tires, engines, and everything else. Some of the cars were turned upside down. We looked through some of the apartments there and the hallways to the apartments were covered with garbage and human waste. All the apartments seemed to have laundry hanging on lines outside their windows. It was interesting for me to see how some people live.

In one case I was assigned, a Brinks truck had been taken over in New York City. Some money orders had been stolen from the truck, and three of them were cashed in the New Haven area. I interviewed people at the three locations where the money orders were cashed and determined that one was cashed by an adult male who used his correct name. I sent the three money orders back to the FBI lab in Washington, DC, and one latent fingerprint was found on each of the three money orders. The Bureau checked the fingerprints against the person who used his correct name and found that one of the prints was his. So I called the man into the FBI office and he came in for an interview.

I asked if he had cashed one of these money orders, and he denied it. But when I showed him the lab report from Washington with one of his fingerprints from one of the stolen money orders, he provided me with a full confession. I asked him where he had gotten the money order, and he gave me the name of another individual.

I checked the second individual's name against the two remaining fingerprints and, sure enough, one of the prints belonged to him. So I called him into the New Haven office and talked to him and, like the first person, he denied having anything to do with it. But when I showed him the lab report with one of his fingerprints from the stolen money order, he also provided me with a full confession.

Then, after he signed the confession, I asked him where he got the money order and he gave me the name of a female. Amazingly enough, when I checked with the fingerprint department, sure enough, the third fingerprint belonged to this individual. Even though several people had handled the money orders in the bank, they were not nervous when they handled the money orders; when people are nervous, they produce excellent fingerprints.

I called the female into the FBI office and, like her cohorts, she denied having anything to do with it. Even when I showed her the lab report with her fingerprint taken from one of the money orders, she continued to deny it and refused to talk to me any longer. As a result, I needed to go to the grand jury before we arrested her and went to trial.

I stayed up most of the night before, reviewing my case and making sure that I knew the serial numbers and the information I needed in order to testify. I went to a small grand jury in New Haven and testified for some time. At the end of the interview, I felt I had done a good job and I stood up to leave, but when I opened the door, it was the wrong door! It was a door to a closet! Talk about humiliation! But the grand jury indicted the woman. She pled guilty and I received three convictions on that case. I realized how fun it was to work with and solve FBI cases.

I was able to work several surveillances for organized crime and obtained a few convictions, apprehended a few fugitives, and had several recoveries. One supervisor had overseen several first office agents in New Haven. We learned a great deal from this supervisor; however, word soon spread among the new agents that if you had a file review with this supervisor, you could expect that he would put one hand upon his head while reviewing your files. If he put two hands on his head while reviewing your files, it meant that he was going to give you a terrible write-up. If there were problems, he would take the agent's paperwork out to the agent's desk and throw it on the desk. He would tell the agent that his work was unacceptable and return to his office without explaining why his work was unacceptable. I was thankful that the supervisor never put more than one hand on his head as he reviewed my file.

On September 17, 1972, our third child was born in New Haven. We named him Brian Daniel Wright. I remember that the doctor who delivered Brian had me next to my wife helping her while he delivered Brian. Karen's parents, Rex and Freda Sutherland, decided to fly to New Haven in order to see their three grandchildren, since they had never been to the East Coast. They flew to New York City from Billings, getting in very late at night, and took a cab to their hotel. During the evening, they heard shots fired in the alley just below them. They found out the next day that someone had been shot in that alley.

That morning we picked up Rex and Freda at their hotel. There was a tremendous storm and the streets of New York City were completely backed up. It took us a great deal of time to get back to our apartment in Cheshire.

We were really glad to have the Sutherlands with us and enjoyed their company. I purchased tickets for them to see the Boston Pops orchestra performing outside the New Haven campus. My father-in-law was the head of the music department at Eastern College in Billings, so he was really looking forward to the concert. Because of the severe rainstorm, however, the concert was cancelled.

After their visit with us, Karen's parents took a taxicab back to the airport. The taxicab driver charged them half as much as their first driver had charged them when they had arrived. They asked the cabdriver how he could charge so much less than the first driver, and he asked, "Did you tell them that you were from out of town?" My father-in-law had told him that they were and that it was the first time they had been to the East Coast. The driver told them that was the reason the first driver had charged them so much.

CHAPTER EIGHT

Transfer to San Francisco

Special agents in the FBI normally receive one office of preference during their bureau career. The office of preference is an office they want to go to, but it often takes years to receive an office of preference. First office agents almost never receive their office of preference for their second office assignment.

I was on surveillance in Bridgeport, Connecticut, with another first office agent who wanted very much to go to San Francisco as a transfer. So he put San Francisco on the office of preference list. I knew I didn't want to go to New York City or Newark, so I put Seattle, Washington, as my office of preference. While the two of us were on this surveillance, we received a radio transmission telling us to call into the New Haven office immediately. The other agent made the first call and came out of the phone booth smiling because he had been transferred to Birmingham, Alabama. I made my call and came out of the phone booth also smiling as I told the other agent I had been transferred to San Francisco.

Since Karen had just delivered our son Brian, I requested and was given a delay of transfer. My final transfer to San Francisco happened close to Christmas day. We had been in New Haven for fifteen months. We decided that Karen and the three children would fly to Salt Lake City, where they would stay with Karen's brother, Alex, and I would drive our Mustang to Salt Lake City to meet them.

The drive was uneventful until I got to Wyoming. It was late at night, and I was driving too fast. The engine suddenly stopped and I drifted over to the side of the road. I had driven that Mustang since it was brand new and would eventually put 269,000 miles on it, and this was the only time the engine simply quit while I was driving. When I pulled the car off to the side of the road, I realized I was on a mountain. The road was on the side of a cliff that went straight down. I decided I'd better drive a little slower.

I checked to see if the car would start and it started right up. I pulled out onto the road and from that point on the highway was covered with black ice. I knew that if I had hit that black ice traveling at the speed I had been driving just a few minutes earlier, I would definitely have gone over the side of the mountain and I would not be alive today. I pulled over to the side of the road again and put my hand over the steering wheel and I remember how my hand shook on that steering wheel, realizing how close I had come to dying. I have never been that nervous at any other time in my life.

I finally arrived in Salt Lake City and picked up Karen and our three children. We then traveled to Merced, California, where I dropped them off with Karen's older brother, Lewis. Then I went into San Francisco and checked into a hotel. Early the next morning I went to the federal building. I got into the elevator and pushed the button for the sixth floor, which at the time was completely occupied by the FBI. Right after I pushed the button, however, another agent got into the elevator and asked, "Are you an agent?" I told him I was. He asked where I went to college and I told him Brigham Young University. "Oh, no, not another Mormon," he said. I took a step toward him and said, "Do you have something against Mormons?" He laughed and said no. He was actually a Mormon bishop and was just giving me a hard time. I was really grateful, because the last thing I needed to do was to get into a fight with another agent on my very first day of work in my new office.

When we got to the sixth floor, I learned that the agent's name was Bob Porter. Bob quickly became my best friend. The squad I worked for was a great squad, and I soon had several friends. Bob Porter took me out to show me various houses where I might live, including a beautiful house in San Ramon for $38,500. I had sold my house in New Jersey for $24,000, so I felt that this home was too expensive. I loved the house, however, and when I showed it to my wife she loved it too, so we decided to buy it after all. While we were waiting to move into the house, we lived in a motel. Our youngest child, Brian, slept in one of the dresser drawers.

San Francisco was a wonderful place to work. You could go to a different restaurant every day for a year, and each one had wonderful food. There were also great sights to see such as the Golden Gate Park, San Francisco Bay, Golden Gate Bridge, Sausalito, the boating industry, Chinatown, the 49ers football team, the Giants baseball team, and the Oakland A's baseball team. There was also Fisherman's Wharf, Alcatraz, and the cable cars, just to mention a few places.

Once Karen and I took the kids down to Hearst Castle in San Simeon. It is amazing how much money was put into that castle. There were statues, swimming pools, gold walls, and chandeliers. Everything you can imagine was found in Hearst Castle. One time, we were looking at a statue and then went on past the swimming pool and up the stairs. At the top of the stairs, we looked back and saw that our son Jimmy was still at the statue. He was amazed because the statue was of an adult male who had no clothes on. We went back and took pictures of Jimmy and then went on with the tour. Everyone should take the opportunity to see Hearst Castle.

The San Francisco office also had the most interesting cases in the country. I spent a good share of my career in the FBI working in foreign counterintelligence. Because of the classified information, I will not be able to recount most of those cases. One of the first cases I worked had to do with a kidnapping of a newborn baby from a hospital in Canada. The FBI received a tip indicating that the child was in a home in Concord, California, a town east of Oakland.

I went out to this house with two other agents, knocked on the door, and we identified ourselves as being FBI. There was no response, so we smashed in the door and found a man and a woman holding a newborn baby. We arrested both the man and the woman and were able to return the baby to his rightful mother in Canada. The case reminded me of why I went into the FBI, and I thought about the Barbara Mackle kidnapping case. I could just imagine how the rightful mother of this baby felt when her child was returned to her.

In 1974, the police chief from the Union City California police department was shot and killed by a Chicano group. The FBI investigated this case, and because a Chicano group was involved, the FBI sent agents who spoke fluent Spanish. Bob Porter and Ray Campos were assigned to be part of this group of agents. Ray Campos was assigned to Bob Porter and they both used the same car.

At the time, Ray Campos did not have a high opinion of The Church of Jesus Christ of Latter-day Saints. After working with Bob for several months, however, he changed his attitude and then had a desire to be baptized into the church. Permission was given for his baptism at Pleasanton, California, and the baptizer was Bob Porter. Bob Porter said the entire baptismal prayer in Spanish and the witnesses had no idea whether he was saying it correctly. After the baptism, I was one of eight FBI agents, all members of the church, who formed a circle around Ray Campos and confirmed him as a member of the church.

I guess that some men will always have that lighthearted desire to play practical jokes on each other. We just can't resist the temptation. It was no different for FBI agents. One of the supervisors in the office was a white male, short and bald. One day while he was away from his office, his agents got into his desk and took out his credentials. (Every agent has a set of credentials with their picture on it.) The agents had a photograph of a member of the Black Panthers. The man was black with a large Afro hairstyle. The agents cut the man's head out of the photograph and put it over the supervisor's photo on his credentials.

Shortly after that, the supervisor returned to his office and retrieved his credentials so he could go interview some people in the San Francisco area. Each time he showed the people his credentials, they would look at him strangely. After a while, the supervisor looked at his credentials and saw the picture and he became quite upset. When the supervisor returned to the FBI office, there probably wasn't an agent from his squad anywhere to be found.

Patty Hearst Kidnapping

One of the most famous FBI cases involved the Patty Hearst kidnapping and her subsequent connection with the Symbionese Liberation Army, or SLA. Donald David DeFreeze organized the SLA while he was at San Quentin Prison. The members of the SLA involved their female friends who visited them in prison and helped the organization from the outside.

In the fall of 1973, two SLA members, Russ Little and Joe Remiro, shot and killed Marcus Foster, the black superintendent of the Oakland schools, with cyanide bullets. Foster's aide was also wounded. The SLA informed the other board members that if the Oakland police did not leave the grounds, the board members would be executed.

In January of 1974, Little and Remiro were arrested and weapons were found in their possession. Their residence in Concord was burned by another SLA member to destroy any evidence, but the FBI nevertheless found a great deal because the building did not burn entirely to the ground.

Donald David DeFreeze, or Cinque, as he was later known, had a lengthy arrest record from one side of this country to the other side. He had been arrested in New Jersey, Ohio, and California. He often escaped lengthy sentences for these arrests by becoming an informant for various law enforcement agencies.

DeFreeze decided that he could free Little and Remiro by kidnapping the daughter of Randolph Apperson Hearst, a wealthy newspaperman, and his wife, Catherine Wood Campbell, and using the girl to barter. On February 4, 1974, three members of the SLA forced their way into an apartment complex in Berkeley, California, and kidnapped Hearst's daughter, Patricia Campbell Hearst, who was a nineteen-year-old Berkeley student. Her fiancé, Steven Weed, was badly beaten during the kidnapping. Patty was then transported to an apartment complex and locked in a small closet, approximately four feet by eight feet; she was in the closet for a long period of time. During this time, she was physically abused and, according to her, raped by SLA members.

The SLA then attempted to trade Patty Hearst for the release of SLA members Russ Little and Joe Remiro, but was unsuccessful. The SLA then demanded that the Hearst family distribute food to every needy Californian. Randolph Hearst was not in the position to do as the SLA demanded, but did donate approximately six million dollars worth of food to the poor in the Bay Area. After the distribution of the food, however, the SLA refused to release Patty Hearst, and later announced in an audio transmission that she had joined their organization and was now known as "Tania." Whatever the SLA's original intent was, many people took advantage of the food distribution, including the Black Panthers, who sold the food at an exorbitant rate to anyone who could pay.

In April of 1974, the SLA robbed the Sunset District branch of the Hibernia Bank in San Francisco, and the bank's surveillance cameras showed Patty Hearst holding an M1 carbine. An arrest warrant was issued for Patricia Hearst in 1975. Patty Hearst issued a statement claiming allegiance to the SLA and referring to her parents and her former fiancé, Steven Weed, as "pigs."

WANTED BY THE FBI

NATIONAL FIREARMS ACT

William Taylor Harris

Date photographs taken unknown
FBI No.: 308,660 L5
Aliases: Mike Andrews, Richard Frank Dennis,
William Kinder, Jonathan Mark, Jonathan Mark
Salamone, Pete
Age: 29, born January 22, 1945, Fort Sill, Oklahoma
(not supported by birth records)
Height: 5'7"   **Eyes:** Hazel
Weight: 145 pounds   **Complexion:** Medium
Build: Medium   **Race:** White
Hair: Brown, short   **Nationality:** American
Occupation: Postal clerk
Remarks: Reportedly wears Fu Manchu type mustache,
may wear glasses, upper right center tooth may be
chipped, reportedly jogs, swims and rides bicycle for
exercise, was last seen wearing army type boots and
dark jacket
Social Security Numbers Used: 315-46-2407,
553-27-8400, 408-48-5467
Fingerprint Classification: 20 L 1 At 12
8 1 U

Emily Montague Harris

Date photographs taken unknown
FBI No.: 325,804 L2
Aliases: Mrs. William Taylor Harris, Mary Hensley,
Joanne James, Anna Lindenberg, Cynthia Sue Mankins,
Dorothy Ann Potri, Emily Montague Schwartz,
Mary Schwartz, Yolanda
Age: 27, born February 11, 1947, Baltimore, Maryland
(not supported by birth records)
Height: 5'3"   **Eyes:** Blue
Weight: 115 pounds   **Complexion:** Fair
Build: Small   **Race:** White
Hair: Blonde   **Nationality:** American
Occupation: Secretary, teacher
Remarks: Hair may be worn one inch below ear level, may
wear glasses or contact lenses; reportedly has partial
upper plate, pierced ears, is a natural food fadist, exercises
by jogging, swimming and bicycle riding, usually wears
slacks or street length dresses, was last seen wearing jeans
and waist length shiny black leather coat; may wear wigs
Social Security Numbers Used: 227-42-2356, 429-42-8000

NATIONAL FIREARMS ACT; BANK ROBBERY

Patricia Campbell Hearst

Date photographs taken unknown
FBI No.: 325,805 L10
Alias: Tania
Age: 20, born February 20, 1954, San Francisco, California
Height: 5'3"   **Eyes:** Brown
Weight: 110 pounds   **Complexion:** Fair
Build: Small   **Race:** White
Hair: Light brown   **Nationality:** American
Scars and Marks: Mole on lower right corner of mouth, scar near right ankle
Remarks: Hair naturally light brown, straight and worn about three
inches below shoulders in length, however, may wear wigs, including
Afro style, dark brown of medium length, was last seen wearing
black sweater, plaid slacks, brown hiking boots and carrying a knife
in her belt

THE ABOVE INDIVIDUALS ARE SELF-PROCLAIMED MEMBERS OF THE SYMBIONESE LIBERATION ARMY AND REPORTEDLY HAVE BEEN IN POS-
SESSION OF NUMEROUS FIREARMS INCLUDING AUTOMATIC WEAPONS. WILLIAM HARRIS AND PATRICIA HEARST ALLEGEDLY HAVE USED GUNS
TO AVOID ARREST. ALL THREE SHOULD BE CONSIDERED ARMED AND VERY DANGEROUS.

Federal warrants were issued on May 20, 1974, at Los Angeles, California, charging the Harrises and Hearst with violation of the National Firearms Act.
Hearst was also indicted by a Federal Grand Jury on June 6, 1974, at San Francisco, California, for bank robbery and use of a weapon during a felony.

**IF YOU HAVE ANY INFORMATION CONCERNING THESE PERSONS, PLEASE NOTIFY ME OR CONTACT YOUR
LOCAL FBI OFFICE. TELEPHONE NUMBERS AND ADDRESSES OF ALL FBI OFFICES LISTED ON BACK.**

C. M. Kelley

DIRECTOR
FEDERAL BUREAU OF INVESTIGATION
UNITED STATES DEPARTMENT OF JUSTICE
WASHINGTON, D. C. 20535
TELEPHONE, NATIONAL, 8-7117

Entered NCIC
Wanted Flyer 475A
September 19, 1974

In the latter part of April 1974, the SLA packed up their weapons and moved their supplies from the Golden Gate Avenue apartment in San Francisco. This was a fortuitous move for them; just after they left their apartment, the FBI discovered it.

The following month, the SLA moved again, this time to Los Angeles, again as the FBI was getting closer to them. SLA members Bill Harris and his wife Emily entered a sporting goods store in Los Angeles, where Bill was caught shoplifting. While store employees were trying to subdue him, Patty Hearst shot several times with her .30 caliber bullets into the front of the store, helping Bill and Emily to escape.

As a result of this event, the Los Angeles Police Department realized that the SLA was in town. The police found six members of the SLA in a house in Los Angeles: Donald DeFreeze, Willie Wolf, Patricia Soltysik, Nancy Ling Perry, Angela Atwood, and Camilla Hall. All six refused to come out of the house and instead used their arsenal against the Los Angeles SWAT team. The entire gun battle was televised, and when the police sent tear gas canisters into the house, it caught on fire. The six SLA members inside died in the fire.

At the time, a reward was offered for the safe return of Patty Hearst, who sent a tape with a message of eulogy for those who died in the fire in Los Angeles. The SLA would continue their fight, she vowed. On April 21, 1975, four members of the SLA held up the Crocker Bank in Carmichael, California and during the robbery, a bank customer was shot and killed.

The FBI worked this case under the code name of HERNAP. The symbol of the SLA was the seven-headed snake. In September of 1975, First Office agents Ray Campos and Jason Moulton found out where Bill and Emily Harris were hiding in San Francisco. They took this information to the special agent in charge of the San Francisco

FBI office and were told to provide more information. Ray Campos and Jason Moulton then took surveillance photographs of the person they believed to be Bill Harris. The photographs were taken back to the office, but there was still uncertainty whether it was indeed Bill Harris, because he had changed the color of his hair and looked very different.

On September 18, 1975, while Bill and Emily Harris were jogging, they were apprehended and placed under arrest by the FBI. Bill Harris was handcuffed with his hands in front of him, in order to take his thumbprint, which immediately identified him. While Emily Harris was being arrested, she used language against the FBI that would make a sailor blush. After Bill and Emily were arrested, the FBI went to 288 Precita in San Francisco, where they discovered bombs and an arsenal of weapons. However, Patty Hearst and another SLA member, Wendy Yoshimura, were not there.

Jason Moulton asked the agents if they had checked 425 Morse Street in San Francisco. They had not. Moulton knew that the press was about to release the information about the Harrises' arrest, and he knew they needed to get to that Morse Street address as soon as possible. Jason Moulton, Tom Padden, and two San Francisco police detectives went there. As they were talking to the owner of the apartment, they heard people talking upstairs. They quickly went upstairs and found Wendy Yoshimura and Patty Hearst. Patty was rushing into another room, it was believed, to retrieve a weapon. The two women were handcuffed and placed under arrest.

Back in 1975, radio transmissions by the FBI were monitored by news agencies. Because of this, when Bill and Emily Harris were taken to the basement of the federal building, several news reporters were there shining their lights and cameras on Bill Harris. Bill Harris immediately raised his hands into the air, which were handcuffed in front of him, and shouted, "Power to the people, power to the people!" I took Bill Harris by one arm and another agent took him by the other arm, and we threw him into the elevator. All of this was filmed by the news media and shown on TV throughout the world. I received telephone calls from people who knew me from the East Coast and from Canada who had seen me on television with Bill Harris. All four individuals, Bill Harris, Emily Harris, Patty Hearst, and Wendy Yoshimura, were booked in the San Francisco office of the FBI.

The trial for Patty Hearst took place in March of 1976. Her lawyer was F. Lee Bailey, who was reportedly paid one million dollars. Patty Hearst's defense was that she was under immediate threat during the entire time from her kidnapping until her arrest. Patty Hearst lost this case. I believe that the reason she lost this case was because she was involved in the bank robbery of the Crocker Bank in Carmichael, where a customer was shot and killed. Another reason I believe she lost this case was because she shot up the sporting goods store in Los Angeles while helping the Harrises to escape. Patty Hearst received a sentence of seven years, of which she served only twenty-two months. President Jimmy Carter commuted her sentence and President Bill Clinton later pardoned her in 2001.

I personally believe that Patty Hearst was brainwashed. Certainly her kidnapping was a legitimate kidnapping and she was terrorized while confined. But I also feel that her sentence was justified. I also understand why her sentence was commuted by President Carter and why she was pardoned by President Clinton. Patty Hearst later married her bodyguard. She is still married to him today and seems to be doing well.

From the time the SLA began, sometime in 1973, the conviction of Patty Hearst on March 11, 1976, all FBI agents in the San Francisco division were required to work many hours on this case each week. Other members of the SLA were sentenced to prison terms, and ultimately all surviving members were arrested. Patty Hearst's abduction caught the attention of the entire world and caused great chaos in the Bay Area.

Although many painful incidents occurred during the Patty Hearst case, there were occasionally some funny events as well. Perhaps it is these occasional humorous moments that help agents maintain their wits about them under exceptionally trying circumstances.

On one occasion, I was asked to investigate a lead in the case in Chinatown. I told the person who assigned me the lead that I did not speak Chinese and he said it didn't matter, that I should get another agent who spoke Chinese to go with me. A good friend of mine, Bob Casper, spoke fluent Cantonese, which he learned in the Monterey language school. Bob consented to go along with me and we went to Grant Avenue in Chinatown. We climbed one flight of stairs to the first apartment and Bob knocked on the door. A man answered the door and Bob spoke to him in Cantonese. The person replied, "I am Korean," which is very unusual in Chinatown. Bob again spoke to him in Cantonese, and again the man said, "I am Korean."

"Bob," I said, "I'm not bilingual, but this man is saying in English that he is Korean." In response, Bob took his credentials out of his jacket pocket and showed them to the individual who peered at Bob's picture. Pointing at the picture, the man said, "I have never seen that man before in my life." I laughed so hard I nearly fell down the steps, although Bob did not see the humor in this.

San Francisco always had plenty of great cases to keep us busy. Four days after Patty Hearst was arrested, President Gerald Ford visited San Francisco. While he was at Union Square, in the heart of San Francisco, Sara Jane Moore tried to shoot him and President Ford came very close to being killed. I worked this case, and if it had not been for an individual who hit Sara Jane just before she fired the shot, President Ford might have been killed. An assassination of the president of the United States just after the Symbionese Liberation Army episode would have been tragic for this nation.

I also helped to provide protection to the Shah of Iran, along with the Secret Service. We had placed pins in our jackets so we could be identified by the Secret Service. The Shah was receiving medical treatment at the Presidio hospital in San Francisco. He was an exciting person who flew his own airplane, had a beautiful wife, and did a lot of good for Iran.

During those years, I was also busy as a husband and father to my growing family. On April 7, 1975, my son, Jerry, was born in Livermore, California, and on March 5, 1977, our last child, Kimberly Ann, was born in Livermore. Cheryl finally had a sister. My children were good kids, and I was grateful to have all of them. At Christmas, my parents would fly out from Philadelphia and we always had a good time together.

My church callings also kept me very busy. From 1973 through 1974, I served in the elder's quorum presidency in San Ramon. Our elder's quorum president was Don McCulley and we became very close friends.

Then, from 1975 through 1978, I became the elder's quorum president for the San Ramon First Ward. We had a wonderful ward and good people kept moving into the ward. One summer we had twenty-one families move into the ward, all of whom fell under the responsibility of the elder's quorum.

Chapter Nine

Work and Play

While working in the San Francisco office, I received a lot of trophies for various sport activities. These trophies came from the FBI, the city of San Francisco, and from the community. Various law enforcement agencies would participate in a softball tournament put on by the FBI and held in South Lake Tahoe each summer.

EIGHT AGENTS WITH TROPHIES

FOUR AGENTS WITH TROPHIES

One summer day we were waiting to start our game, when the left fielder walked to the pitcher's mound from left field then fell over unconscious on the mound. The left fielder was from the Alameda, California police department. One of the members of his team looked at him, turned him over, and said, "He's fine. He'll be all right." However, one agent's wife was a nurse and she insisted that an ambulance be called. While traveling in the ambulance to the hospital, the police officer died. It was a solemn reminder to me that when you say that someone is all right, you had better know what you are talking about.

That same afternoon it began snowing, which was hard to believe since it was August. On the way home from the game, an agent and his wife, who was a nurse, came across a huge accident on the Benicia Bridge in northern California. The woman rushed up to a man who was suffocating in his own blood and was able to save his life. She later said that she was going to stop going to these softball tournaments because it was a lot safer being a nurse in the hospital.

One time I played in a game for the FBI, and while we were sitting on the bleachers waiting to play, below the bleachers a law enforcement officer from South Lake Tahoe was arresting a person for being drunk and disorderly. All the law enforcement officers in the stands were heckling the officer and telling him everything he was doing wrong. He didn't take the kidding with a friendly smile and it finally got to the point that he threw the person in the back of the police car and then quickly drove off.

It was fun playing in the tournaments, and I remember presenting the special agent in charge, or SAC, from San Francisco with a trophy that we won. It was amazing how many law enforcement officers participated in the tournaments, with teams coming to play from as far away as Los Angeles.

SOFTBALL TEAM WITH THE SAC - SAN FRANCISCO

One time I went to the Tuolumne River to go fishing with five other agents from my squad in San Francisco. We traveled across some land owned by one of the agents' parents. To get to the river, it was necessary to travel straight down a very steep slope. As we were coming down the mountains, we saw various homes, which had been carved into the rocks by the Chinese. The Chinese apparently had lived and worked there in the past. When we got down to the river, I saw a large rock about the size of an automobile. It was half in the river and half on the land. I decided to jump up on the rock, and as I was leaving the land to jump, I saw a giant rattlesnake coiled up on the rock exactly where I was going to land. I veered to the right and landed on my back on a rock pile. The other agents stood looking at me like I was crazy. I took my .22 revolver from my hip and lined it up with the rattlesnake. As his head was moving back and forth in a hypnotic trance, I followed it with my gun and blew it off.

What was left of him fell on the land below the rock. I went over to the snake and realized how big it was. It had thirteen rattles.

I asked the agent, whose parents owned the land, if he had ever seen any snakes. He told me that he had been there many, many times and had never seen a snake. When I shot the rattlesnake, he told me that if you see one snake then there is always a second snake close by. That really ruined my fishing that day, since I kept looking around me while I was casting to see if there were any other snakes.

The Dan White/Mayor George Moscone Case

In the late 1970s, a city councilman named Dan White, who had formerly worked in the San Francisco police department, turned in his resignation. Then he changed his mind and decided not to resign. However, Mayor George Moscone would not give him his position back, and White was not allowed to withdraw his resignation. White became so upset over this incident that he shot and killed Mayor Moscone and Harvey Milk, another councilman. White then went to trial over this incident and his attorney used the "Twinkie Defense." His attorney said that White was always eating Twinkies, which affected his mind. It surprised everyone that the jury accepted White's story and he was set free. As a result of White being set free, one hundred thousand people began a protest at City Hall in San Francisco, just one block from the Federal Building, which houses the FBI. The protestors marched from the city hall to the federal building on Golden Gate Avenue, blocking Turk Street and Golden Gate Avenue.

I could see the protestors from the sixth floor of the federal building as they threw paint on the buildings, broke windows, and even burned up police cars. The police clubbed some protestors and I watched as the police marched down Elm Street. At the same time, the police marched down Golden Gate Avenue until they had a group of protestors surrounded on Polk Street. The police then took the protestors and threw them into vans to be transported to jail. Included here are two photographs taken of this protest, which was widely reported throughout the country.

RIOTERS IN SAN FRANCISCO

RIOTERS BEING CLUBBED BY POLICE

The Soviet Consulate in San Francisco is located at 2790 Green Street. While I was working in San Francisco, several demonstrations took place outside the Soviet Consulate. One day when I was working as a complaint agent, I received a call from the Soviet Consulate about a protest that was in progress. I asked the caller what the protesters were doing and he said that they were marching around the consulate. I told him that they had the right as American citizens to protest as long as they were not doing anything illegal. He told me that if they had been protesting in Russia they would have immediately been thrown into prison.

One day, another protest was being held outside the Soviet Consulate and one of the protesters threw blood onto the building. Inasmuch as this was a violation of the law, I went down to the consulate and observed the hundreds of people protesting and the many San Francisco police officers at the scene. The San Francisco Tactical (TAC) Squad members were wearing high boots and a couple of officers were on horses. I was talking to an officer and he asked me if I would like to see the crowd dispersed. I told him it would be nice to see that happen. The police officers began pounding the street with their boots and moving their horses, and the protesters began running away from the consulate, down the hill. They apparently thought that the police officers on horses were chasing them. I was amazed to see how efficient and well trained the San Francisco police department was.

As a note of interest, on top of the building of the Soviet Consulate were large wooden boxes. Some of these boxes contained instruments used to monitor telephone conversations taking place in San Francisco. The Soviets would use words such as "FBI" or "intelligence" to trigger conversations with Americans. The Soviets claimed to the media that the wooden boxes were used for storage items.

In later years, I would sometimes interview immigrants from Eastern Bloc countries because the Russian KGB would often make demands of them in order for them to come to this country. One day, I was interviewing a Romanian immigrant and I mentioned Safeway stores. The immigrant then began to cry, and I couldn't understand what I had done wrong. I asked her if there was something that I had said that caused her to cry. She looked at me and said that in Romania you could never get fresh fruit. She remembered waiting in long lines on the street corner where potatoes were dumped in the gutter and were then claimed by those in line. I think that we often don't realize what we have when we live in this country.

On March 30, 1976, I requested and was assigned to the Oakland Resident Agency, working Chinese and Middle Eastern matters. I asked for the Oakland Resident Agency because it was much closer to my home. Bob Porter was also assigned to the Oakland Resident Agency, and we became even closer friends. One day Bob and I were in a Bureau car together and we passed several prostitutes on the side of the road. The prostitutes were dressed in their normal attire and motioned us to come over to see them. Bob began singing a religious song, and after we drove past the prostitutes, I asked him why he was singing. He told me that if you sing a religious song, you could keep only one thought in your head at a time.

I worked with Bob Porter on one of the cases assigned to him involving a drug addict who was a fugitive. Back in the 1970s, people were paid money for donating their blood. Drug addicts would often donate their blood and lie about using drugs in order to be paid. They would then take the money to buy illegal drugs and shoot them into their arm. Bob's fugitive made arrangements with the blood bank to donate blood and Porter found out about it. We informed the people at the blood bank about the situation. We planned to arrest him after he gave blood, while he was weak. After the blood was taken from the fugitive, they pulled the needle out of his arm, and Bob and I grabbed and cuffed him. This was the easiest arrest I have ever been involved in.

FBI agents were often called to serve on juries, but police officers were never called to jury duty. I could never understand why this was the case, because when the defense attorney would find out that we worked for the FBI, we would immediately be released from jury duty. Nevertheless, for some unknown reason, FBI agents were not considered to be police officers and were, therefore, considered eligible for jury duty.

Once, when I was called for jury duty, the potential jurors were asked if anyone knew a police officer. It was obvious that the defense attorney would release me, so I decided to have some fun. In response to his question, two of us raised our hands. The defense attorney questioned the first person, and then turned to me and asked me who I knew in law enforcement. I knew hundreds of people there, I told him.

When he asked me how I could possibly know that many people in law enforcement, I responded that I was an FBI agent. He immediately kicked me off the jury.

On another occasion, the question was asked if anyone had ever testified at a trial or grand jury. I raised my hand. The defense attorney asked me when I had testified and I told him that I had testified on numerous occasions. He asked me how that was possible and I told him that I was an FBI agent. The defense attorney dismissed me from the jury. It was easy to see that FBI agents would never serve on a jury, and I didn't understand why the state of California called us to jury duty in the first place.

In April of 1976, I received a QSI, which is a financial reward for doing a good job. It was a real surprise to me, and the reason I received it was because of my development of informants in Middle Eastern matters. I also received a letter from FBI Director, Clarence M. Kelly, regarding this QSI. QSIs are great incentive awards for agents because they raise you a step in grade and that step always stays with you, even after retirement. In July of 1976, I received my grade 12 salary increase.

CHAPTER TEN

Kidnapping—Innocent Victims

The Chowchilla Kidnapping Case

After a long day at school, twenty-six children were on their way home in a bus driven by Ed Ray. It was a hot, humid day on July 15, 1976. They lived in Chowchilla, California, a small farming community. The children, ages five to fourteen, were eager to get home, grab a snack, and shake off the doldrums of school. The older ones probably had unwanted chores waiting while the younger children had visions of running, biking, and just being carefree kids. Their plans were rudely interrupted when Ed suddenly stopped the school bus after seeing an older white van supposedly broken down on the side of the road. He opened the door of the bus to offer help, and a man with two guns and a nylon stocking mask over his head suddenly appeared and entered the bus. The masked gunman ordered the driver and the children to move to the back of the bus.

Two more masked men quickly walked from behind the white van and entered the bus. As the frightened children watched in horror, the masked men drove them off in the bus with the white van following. Sometime later, they stopped where another white van was parked. The children and driver were separated into two groups and loaded into the two vans. There was no escape. The vans were securely locked.

The hungry, frightened children and the bus driver huddled together in the vans for what seemed like hours. They were driven approximately one hundred miles to Livermore.

The vans abruptly stopped and the bus driver and the tired children were ordered out of the vans. The bus driver was stripped of his pants and boots, then they were all forced to climb into an opening in the top of a moving van that had been buried beneath the ground in a stone quarry.

The children were appeased a little with fruit juice, dry cereal, and water, which had been left in the moving van for them. There were mattresses and fans attached to a battery. It was dark and scary in the van with no noticeable way to escape. They desperately wanted out and started piling up the mattresses. The driver and some of the older children were able to reach the opening in the roof. There was a metal lid covering the hole. Ed, the bus driver, tried to move the metal lid but it wasn't easy. Something heavy was weighing it down. As he slowly moved the metal lid, he discovered an industrial size battery on top. There was also dirt and debris piled on top of the opening to camouflage the area. As the night air filled their lungs and their eyes adjusted, the kidnap victims saw brilliant stars covering the dark sky. They quietly and carefully lifted a small boy up to the surface to determine if anyone was watching them. It was quiet. They were alone. After being in the ground for approximately sixteen hours, they all climbed safely out of the moving van to freedom.

During this time, there were frantic parents waiting to find out what had happened to their children who had never arrived home from school. The abandoned bus had been discovered and law enforcement officers were at work with very few clues to lead them to the missing children. The bus driver and the children walked through the quarry and eventually came across two workers. The workers were not aware of the kidnapping. They pulled out a pair of coveralls for Ed and called the police. The self-rescued hostages were taken to the Santa Rita Rehabilitation Center where health care workers examined and fed them.

The rock quarry was approximately eight miles from my home so I was told to go to the center to meet and interview some of the children who had been kidnapped. Some of the younger children were emotionally affected by the kidnapping, and I noticed one child about six years old lying in a fetal position sucking her thumb. The older students were excellent witnesses, however, and described the suspects and their clothing, belt buckles, and nicknames. I was very impressed with the things they said.

The next day, Special Agent Frank Doyle went down into the moving van, which had previously held the captives, and within a few seconds he was covered in sweat. I thought how lucky the children were to live through this incident. They could have died a horrible death had they not escaped. They certainly were fortunate to have had the bus driver with them. One day and a half after the kidnapping, the bus driver and the twenty-six students were returned to Chowchilla to be with their families.

The three kidnappers were later identified as Rick Schoenfeld, his older brother, Jim Schoenfeld, and a friend of theirs named Fred Woods. All three of these individuals were from wealthy families. Fred Wood's father owned the rock quarry in Livermore where the children had been buried.

Since the kidnappers did not take the victims out of California, the kidnapping was not a federal violation. The FBI continued to work the case closely with the local police departments under the Police Cooperation Act. The kidnappers had planned to demand five million dollars ransom for the return of the children, but they could not get through to the Chowchilla police department because there were so many people calling in and out of the office at the time. Before the kidnappers could make their demands known, the media had reported that the bus driver and children had been rescued.

The three young kidnappers decided to make a run for it. Fred Woods flew to Vancouver, Canada, and checked into a hotel using an assumed name. Jim Schoenfeld tried on two occasions to drive into Canada. He was turned down at the border because he lied to border agents, and then was turned down a second time because border agents found a gun in his car that had been left there by Woods. Jim Schoenfeld was lucky the border guards didn't place him under arrest for the gun violation. At the same time, Rick Schoenfeld felt guilty and returned to his parents' home in or near Atherton to confess to his parents about the kidnapping and surrender to the police.

After Rick confessed, Fred Woods and Jim Schoenfeld came under suspicion. Ed Ray, the bus driver, was placed under hypnosis and was able to provide additional information regarding the kidnapping. Jim had told Fred Woods he would meet him at a post office in Vancouver and bring money for them both to use during their escape.

With this information, the FBI was asked to use the Unlawful Flight to Avoid Persecution Act to track down these two men.

After being turned down trying to cross the border, Jim got rid of his car and purchased an old truck. He later headed toward home in California. While driving on Highway 101 south of San Francisco, a stranger in another vehicle saw Jim in his truck and recognized him from photos being shown to the public on TV. The stranger pulled off Highway 101, found a California highway patrol officer, and told him what he had seen. The officer was able to catch up to Jim Schoenfeld and place him under arrest.

By this time, Fred Woods was getting worried waiting for Jim, who had said that he would bring money up to Vancouver. Jim had instructed Fred to go to a certain post office in Vancouver two different times each day until they could be reunited. Since Fred was getting nervous about Jim not showing up, he wrote a letter to a friend of his in California using his false name and saying not to tell anyone about the letter. The friend, however, immediately took the letter to the FBI and the information was sent to the Royal Canadian Mounted Police (RCMP), who then arrested Woods.

I thought it was very interesting to see how various agencies, such as the FBI, the Alameda County Sheriff's Office, the Chowchilla Sheriff's Office, the Santa Clara Sheriff's Office, the RCMP, the Vancouver British Columbia Police, the California Highway Patrol, and other police departments and agencies around the world could work so closely together to bring about such a good conclusion. This case shows clearly how law enforcement agencies can and should work together. It is also interesting to note that all three of the kidnappers were arrested within two weeks after the actual kidnapping.

After their arrests, the kidnappers met again in a small courtroom in Chowchilla, where they all initially pled not guilty. After a change in venue from Chowchilla to Alameda County in northern California, on July 25, 1977, the three individuals pled guilty to twenty-seven counts of kidnapping for ransom without inflicting injury. Initially all three of the individuals were sentenced to life in prison without the possibility of parole. In 1981, this was changed to life with the possibility of parole. The three kidnappers have been in prison for over thirty years and are still trying to get out. They have attempted to gain parole, but each attempt has been turned down. The last attempt was made in January of 2009. I believe that the reason they have been turned down each time was because of the lack of concern each of them had for the children, and because each child came close to a horrible death. It will probably never be fully known how this kidnapping affected the lives of each of the children.

A final note on this case: Case agents are the ones in charge of the investigations. In the Chowchilla kidnapping, LeRoy Teitsworth was the case agent and was instrumental in providing valuable information about this case.

CHAPTER ELEVEN

Bank Robbery Cases

I arrested many perpetrators while assigned to investigating bank robberies. It is funny how some bank robbers would say, "I will never be taken alive." Then when faced with several agents with shotguns, they say, "Don't shoot, don't shoot," and hold up their hands.

At that time, four of us from Oakland were investigating bank robberies. The FBI prosecuted all bank robberies. It is not the same today—many bank robberies are prosecuted by the local police departments.

One of the cases assigned to me involved an individual who worked in the infirmary giving shots at the Alameda County naval base. He made the mistake of robbing a bank that was located a half block from the FBI office.

I was the first agent to arrive at the bank and just missed the robber. I asked the victim teller if the bank robber had left the note on her counter. She told me that he had. Bank robbers often leave notes saying they will kill someone, trying to get the tellers nervous enough to give up all their money.

So I had the counter dusted for prints, picked up the surveillance film, and interviewed the teller. The teller told me that the bank robber had got into line and waited for his turn and then came up to her window. He handed her a demand note, but at the time he was holding a savings account book in his other hand so that he would look like a customer. (Most banks today don't require that customers keep savings accounts books.)

The teller had just started to read the demand note when the robber pulled the note from her hand. She said, "If you want any money from me, you have to let me read the note," and she pulled the note out of his hand along with the savings account book. The bank robber pulled out a gun and said, "Give me the money or I will kill you." She gave him a bundle of money and he ran out of the bank, leaving the savings account book from another bank with the teller.

I took the savings account book and went to the other bank, where I found out who the account was registered to. That person had an arrest record and I was able to get his mug shot. I put it in a photo spread and went back to show the photos to the teller I'd interviewed, as well as to another teller at the bank. The first teller identified the robber, but the second teller said she didn't think it was the man.

I went to the U.S. attorney to get a warrant to arrest the bank robber, but he refused to give me one, saying I didn't have enough evidence. We then had to put the robber under surveillance and wait for him to rob another bank. I was able to get writing samples produced by the subject from the Alameda County military base, and took them to a handwriting expert. He told me that the person who wrote the demand note was also the person who wrote individual files for the infirmary. I took this information to the U.S. attorney, and this time he authorized approval for the arrest. We arrested the individual and took him into Oakland Resident Agency where I interviewed him.

Almost every bank robber who I have ever arrested has given me a signed statement. This individual, however, refused to admit anything. Because of the late hour, we put him in the Oakland police department jail, and that night I got a search warrant for his property out at the Alameda military base where he lived. Another agent and I served a search warrant on New Year's Eve and we went with some of the military security out to his residence. We found the jacket with paint stains on the sleeve that he used during the robberies, the stainless steel automatic weapon that he used during the robberies, and three folded- up wads of money that were taken from the three banks he had previously robbed. We checked the prerecorded Federal Reserve notes and found that all of the Federal Reserve notes were in these packets. So we seized all of these items, and the next morning the other agent and I picked up the bank robber to take him to San Francisco for arraignment. I sat in the back seat with the man and asked if he was ready to confess. He said that he was not.

I told him that we had served a search warrant at his residence and had seized his gun, clothing, and three rolls of money, which had the prerecorded Federal Reserve notes. I also advised him that we had confiscated a cassette, which I had listened to and learned that he was talking about each of the robberies he had committed. This individual was a black male who was trying to save up enough money to start a black militant organization. I then took the robber to arraignment, where the judge released him on his own recognizance, that is, let him go free. I had never had a bank robber allowed to go free before; judges have always put very high bail on these bank robbers.

The bank robber immediately returned to the base and took his property from the base and went AWOL. The next thing I knew, the robber was down in Albuquerque, New Mexico, and had robbed a bank, using a taxicab to make his getaway. When he ran out of the bank with a .22 pistol, he jumped in the taxicab, put the gun to the driver's head, and told him to drive away in a hurry. Agents responding to the bank saw him put the gun to the taxicab driver's head and they followed him in two different FBI vehicles. The taxicab stopped on the side of the road and the robber ran out and hid behind some bushes as the cab drove off. The agents saw the bank robber run into the bushes and started moving in on him. They yelled to the man to come out or he would be shot.

The robber came out of the bushes and put the .22 to his head, telling the agents not to come any closer or he would shoot himself. The agents went closer and he did shoot himself in the head. But because he did not have the .38 stainless steel special that I had previously seized, he injured himself, but did not die. The bank robber was considered no longer mentally competent to stand trial, thus I didn't even get a conviction despite all of the work I had done on this case.

Another bank robbery case assigned to me involved a bank robber who came up to Oakland from southern California and was arrested in Emeryville, California. I interviewed him and he gave me a signed statement. This man then went to trial in southern California, and I had to fly down there to testify in the case. When I took the stand, the defense attorney, or DA, asked me if I was a special agent of the FBI, and I told him that I was. He then said, "What makes you so special?" He wanted to rattle me, but it didn't work.

Next, the DA asked me if I knew that the bank robber hadn't eaten for a couple of days while he was in jail. I told him that I had no knowledge that he had not eaten. The DA asked me how I knew the bank robber had robbed the bank. I showed him the statement signed by the bank robber. As I was leaving the stand, the defense attorney said he was willing to accept that the man did rob the bank, but said that the man had been suffering from alcoholic blackout. It took the jury almost no time to come back with a guilty verdict.

I had another bank robbery assigned to me that involved a couple of bank robbers who used Uzis and had been arrested before. I located their residence, which was close to the FBI office, and we went there early in the morning to arrest them. (The FBI goes early because over eighty-five percent of bank robbers in Oakland are drug addicts who do not get up early in the morning.) I told one of the agents to cover the back door and asked Agent John Rowland to kick in the front door. John had a good reputation for kicking in doors, but in this attempt he missed the hardware on the door and got his size fifteen shoe caught in the door. "I'm stuck," he said, "and I can't get out."

At that point a woman answered the door and we rushed in, leaving Rowland still stuck in the door. We arrested one man, who was still in bed. We asked him where the other bank robber was, and he said he wasn't there. We found all kinds of evidence, but not the other bank robber. Surveillance was set up on the residence and I waited outside in a car.

A taxicab pulled up and a patron in the car looked up at the place and then was driven off. I said I would check to make sure that the patron was not the other bank robber. I got to the cab, had the person get out of the back seat, and looked him over. He didn't look anything like the bank robber, so I told him he could go. The next day, I received a call from an informant, who asked me why the FBI let the person go who was in the back of the cab. I really felt stupid and I didn't tell the other agents what I had done. The informant then told me where the other bank robber was and we took off in three different cars to the location. En route, I saw the bank robber going past in the other direction with someone else driving the car. I immediately told the other agents; we all did U-turns and headed off the car. I pulled the driver out of the car, threw him on the hood of the car and cuffed him. The other agents pulled the bank robber out of the car, and cuffed him.

We took him down to the office and placed him under arrest. I was very grateful we caught him because I wouldn't have been able to live with the fact that I'd found him and let him go without realizing who he was.

Another bank robbery case that was assigned to me involved the Bank of America in Oakland. The three robbers went into the bank and used weapons. They told the customers to lie down on the floor, and then they went into the vault, cleaned it out, and escaped in a stolen car. We recovered the stolen car about a half a mile from the bank, but no one saw which direction the robbers had gone. Their team consisted of two black males and one Hispanic male.

Eventually we arrested the two black males, and learned that they had believed their Hispanic partner was holding out on them regarding the loot from the bank. They had taken him to a high hill in San Francisco, where they gagged him, beat him up, shot him in the head, and then threw him off the cliff. That was one conviction I wouldn't get for that bank robbery.

One of the bank robbers was a really evil man who had previously committed another murder and had gotten away with it. The U.S. attorney called me to his office and said he wanted me to talk to the defense attorney with him. The District attorney said his client would plead guilty to unarmed robbery. It is important to know that, at the time, unarmed robbery carried a maximum sentence of twenty years, while armed robbery carried a maximum sentence of twenty-five years. I told the U.S. attorney, in front of the defense, that we would be crazy to accept the guilty plea of unarmed robbery when I had pictures of the bank robbers putting their weapons in the faces of the tellers, and even taking purses away from the customers in the bank.

The U.S. attorney took me aside and said, "Look, Jim, a bird in the hand is worth two in the bush." I couldn't believe that he was letting the robber off and was willing to accept the unarmed robbery plea.

In the same case, there was also a motion to suppress hearing that was held in regard to the bank robbers, and I had to testify. After I testified and sat down, the judge looked down at the robber and said, "Unfortunately for you, you took a very good picture at the bank." He then spoke to the man's lawyer, "And you wasted our time with this motion to suppress, because everything is accepted."

I then spoke to the individual who prepares the reports for the judge prior to sentencing. I told her what an animal the bank robber was, that he had committed two known murders, had a long rap sheet, and was just waiting to kill another person. She made out a scorching report for the judge. On the day of the sentencing, I went to the court to see what would happen.

The judge looked down at the bank robber and said, "You are not fit for society and should never be allowed to be in society." He said he could only sentence him to twenty years because that was the maximum allowable, otherwise he would have given him a longer sentence.

When the bank robber realized what was happening, he got up out of his seat and said, "I will never go to jail for twenty years." A glass pitcher of water was on the table where the robber and his lawyer were seated. The man picked up the pitcher and threw it at the marshals coming to subdue him. Two marshals grabbed him and they rolled around the courtroom as he punched one of them. They finally cuffed him and dragged him out of the courtroom. The bank robber received another five years for assaulting a federal officer and, justifiably, got his twenty-five-year sentence. That was a happy day for me, because I got a very dangerous person off the street.

I remember one case that involved a female who robbed several different banks. For each robbery, she wore a different outfit and wig so she looked very different in the surveillance photos taken. When we finally identified her and arrested her, we served a search warrant out to her house and were able to recover the outfits she wore during the robberies.

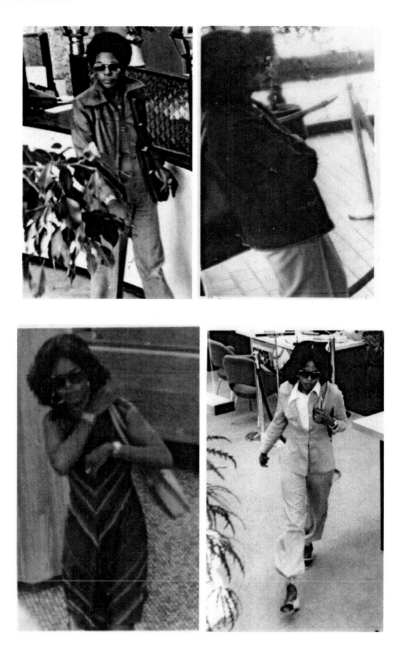

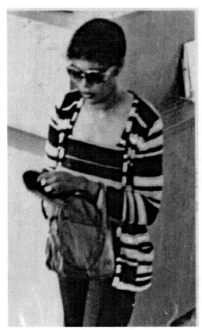 

FEMALE BANK ROBBER

In another case, I had a warrant for a female who lived in Oakland. The FBI had begun hiring female agents and, in this particular situation, I was especially grateful to have one with me in making this arrest. We entered the home and found the woman with her husband. She was wearing a sexy nightgown and it was clear that we'd interrupted them. The female agent took the woman into another room, had her get dressed, and then cuffed her. We were then able to take the suspect back for booking. Had I not been assigned a female agent at the time, I would have wrapped a blanket around the woman and taken her in, but might well have had difficulties with her husband. As it was, we had no problems at all.

One case involved a bank robber who was known as the "handkerchief bandit" because he wore a handkerchief over his face during his robberies. This man was very good at what he did—he had committed twenty-seven bank robberies. We finally found him and we arrested him and his girlfriend. They appeared before two different judges, and she received a longer sentence than he did. He certainly got off easy for robbing twenty-seven banks. Sometimes the justice system just isn't very fair.

Bank robbers are not usually known to be the most intelligent people in the world. One reason for this is that, in many cases, bank robbers are drug addicts. One case took place in a bank very close to the FBI office in Oakland. The robber had left the bank with the money, but had left his demand note on the counter. I found the demand note and asked the teller if the robber had left it, and she said that he had. When I turned the note over, I saw that it was written on the back of a Pacific Gas and Electric bill. Although it was hard to believe that anybody could be this dumb, I thought we'd better check it out. The next day, we arrested the robber. Sure enough, he had used his own Pacific Gas and Electric bill on which to write the demand note.

Then there was the bank robber who went into a Wells Fargo Bank on Broadway Street in Oakland and gave the demand note to the teller. Demand notes usually say things like, "Give me the money or I will kill you." When the teller read his note, she looked at him and said, "If you want any money out of me, you will sit down and wait for me to get it." In compliance with the teller's demand, the man sat down. The teller then hit the alarm, and within a couple of minutes police officers were rushing into the bank. When the police officers asked the teller, "Which way did he go?", she indicated that the robber was sitting right there. That was one of the Oakland police department's easiest arrests.

In another bank robbery, an elderly man took an automatic weapon and put it in the face of the teller. I got to the bank right after he left, just missing him. But I was able to get good pictures from the bank surveillance camera and immediately determined the bank robber's identity. He was also very easy to find since he had been arrested for bank robbery several years before.

I went to the home of the robber's sister and told her that her brother had better turn himself in because the police might shoot and kill him. The next day, the sister came to the FBI office in Oakland and said her brother was here to see Jim Wright. I walked out of my office, and sure enough, there was the sister with her brother, the bank robber. I frisked him, interviewed him, and he gave me a signed statement. When I asked him why he had robbed the bank, he said he'd done it because he wanted to go back to jail. He was fed three meals a day there and had all of his needs met.

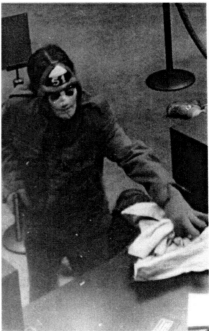

TWO BANK ROBBERS NEVER IDENTIFIED

BANK ROBBER REACHING FOR HIS GUN WHILE
CONFRONTING THE BANK MANAGER

One day, I was working in the Oakland Resident Agency when an unidentified individual called me to say that the savings and loan was giving one thousand dollar rewards to people who identified bank robbers. I told the person I could also get him a thousand dollars for the identity of a bank robber, but I would need to verify that the individual named was indeed a bank robber.

I met the would-be informant at an undisclosed location in Oakland, and he told me his daughter had robbed two or three banks, then he gave me her name. I told him that in order to receive the full reward he needed to give me more than one bank robber. So the man gave me the names of the two other individuals who had robbed the banks with his daughter. When I identified the three individuals, I realized he had told me the truth. In a very short period of time, we were able to arrest all three individuals. I then took the thousand dollars out from the

Savings and Loan and gave the money to the person who provided the names of the bank robbers.

Two other cases are worth mentioning here, although they involved stolen merchandise rather than stolen cash. On May 2, 1977, five hundred cases of Folgers coffee were stolen from an ICX terminal in Hayward, California. Seventy subjects were identified and 185 cases valued at $19,500 were recovered. Also recovered were ten radios and various other items.

Later that year, on October 24, two million dollars worth of precious stones were stolen in Seattle, Washington. I had the opportunity to work on this case. Ultimately, ninety-seven percent of the stolen stones were recovered and six people were arrested.

During the five years I worked bank robberies, from 1976 to 1981, I was able to arrest many robbers, most of whom were drug addicts. After arresting the culprits, I would interview them and get a signed statement from them. Then I would do something different from the other agents working bank robberies. I would ask the robbers about their life. I heard many interesting stories that way and could see why many of them had become bank robbers.

One year, most of the bank robbers I arrested had targeted savings and loan associations. That year I arrested fifteen robbers. Did I get some dangerous people off the street? Yes, I did, and I am very proud of it. That year members of the California Savings and Loan Association were meeting in San Francisco and asked that I come speak to them about bank security. I prepared a speech to give during their luncheon. After eating lunch, I was introduced to all of the various members of the association. When I went up to the podium to begin my speech on how to protect savings and loans, a man came up behind me, put his arm around me and said, "You are not here to talk to us. You are here to be honored because of the many savings and loan bank robbers that you arrested." Then he presented me with a plaque which said I was being honored for outstanding service as a law enforcement officer. I was very grateful for this honor.

Stew Ivie's Move

In 1976, my best friend, Stew Ivie, moved to San Ramon and became a neighbor. Stew was a U.S. postal inspector, and we worked cases involving individuals who would rob post offices and banks. Stew supervised the postal inspectors.

Seeing a blue Mustang that had been seized in a drug investigation, Stew commented on a couple of occasions that he would like to try the Mustang just to see how it drove. So Stew was given the keys to the Mustang and drove it from Oakland to his home in San Ramon and parked it in the driveway.

Stew didn't realize that the postal inspectors had previously seized a different blue Mustang. During the early morning hours, one of the other postal inspectors drove the other Mustang, which looked exactly like the first Mustang, out to Stew's residence. The two Mustangs were switched, and the other postal inspectors set up across the street to see how Stew would react. Expecting to have some fun, they also videotaped it.

Stew came out of his house and tried opening the doors to the Mustang with negative results. He tried to open the trunk, but again with negative results. Next, he went into his garage where he could be seen using a file on the keys.

At that moment, another postal inspector drove up and told Stew he needed help on a case. Stew went with him and while he was gone, the postal inspectors traded the Mustangs back. When Stew returned, he tried the keys again. This time the driver's door opened right up. He tried the trunk and the passenger door, and each of these opened right up, to his complete surprise. Why hadn't the keys worked before? It was a mystery.

Stew returned the Mustang to work and the postal inspectors never told him what they had done.

When Stew retired from the postal service in November of 1992, he had a party at one of the nicer restaurants in San Francisco. The restaurant was filled with postal inspectors, who were friends of Stew's from several states, and several members of his family as well. The retirement dinner consisted of the best food you could imagine.

I had been asked to speak, so I stood up and told the postal inspectors, most of them armed with weapons, that I worked bank robberies for the FBI. In fact, I had worked bank robberies from November of 1976 through February of 1981. I said that one time I arrested a bank robber and interviewed him to get his signed statement. I asked him why he had robbed a bank and told him that it would be much easier to rob a post office. The reason he shouldn't rob a bank was because banks have armed guards, prerecorded Federal Reserve notes, tear gas packets, and surveillance cameras. If he robbed post offices, however, it would be much easier. I told him that postal inspectors were kindly old men who never carried weapons.

As I said this, all of the postal inspectors looked at me as if they wanted to kill me, but I hadn't finished my story yet. I said that I had arrested another bank robber and asked him why he robbed a bank. He said that he had previously robbed post offices, but had been arrested by a postal inspector named Stew Ivie. Stew told him that he should rob banks instead of post offices, because bank robberies were investigated by special agents of the FBI, who were kindly old men who never carried weapons. The audience laughed and I presented Stew with a letter from the FBI Special Agent in Charge of San Francisco honoring him for his work on postal and bank robberies with the FBI. The next speaker was an inspector who told the group about the blue Mustang and showed the videotape of Stew filing the keys and how the cars were changed. It was a complete surprise to Stew that he had been set up. We all had a good laugh over this. The inspectors had a great time that evening.

CHAPTER TWELVE

Jim Jones and the People's Temple

Tragedy in Guyana

I was working for the Oakland Resident Agency, involved in some of the biggest cases in the history of the Bureau. One case concerned the Reverend James Warren Jones, a.k.a. Jim Jones, and the People's Temple. The People's Temple is mainly remembered for the tragedy that took place November 18, 1978, at Port Kaituma, Georgetown, Guyana, also known as Jonestown, where over nine hundred members of the Temple committed suicide. Almost a third of those who died were children.

In 1954, Jones started his own church and, in 1955, named it the People's Temple Full Gospel Church. Jones faked a number of healings to increase his members' faith and to raise money. He was also involved in several charity efforts in order to recruit poor people, and he earned a reputation for helping the homeless and drug addicts. In reality, his "gospel" was actually communism. Jones had rejected the Bible and turned away from Christianity.

By the 1970s, he owned over a dozen locations in California, had nearly five thousand members, and opened the People's Temple in San Francisco on Geary Boulevard. Jones's political power continued to grow because of the influence he could exert by telling his members to vote for certain candidates. He had meetings with important political figures, including (before they held office) San Francisco mayor George Moscone, Vice President Walter Mondale, and First Lady Rosalynn Carter, to mention a few. Jones received support from political candidates including Assemblyman Willie Brown and Moscone. He also told his people to vote for certain political candidates, and in return for helping Moscone get elected mayor, was appointed chairman of the San Francisco Housing Commission.

There were, however, concerns about the People's Temple. Complaints had been made that people turned over their houses and possessions to the Reverend Jones. Then, after giving Jones everything they owned, he put them out on the street selling bread to make additional money. Complaints were also made about Jones's "angels" who forced people to do things they didn't want to do. The angels passed baskets on long sticks in the People's Temple collecting donations. After the collection, Jones would stand at the pulpit and count the money. If he didn't get enough, he would point at people and claim to put a hex on them, which scared them to death. He would then send his angels out again with their baskets and, by this time, the people were throwing in everything they had, including watches and wallets.

Permission from Jones was required for people to have sex, even if they were married. During one of the services held in San Francisco, a teenage girl was accused of having sex without Jones's permission.

Jones took the girl and, in front of the whole congregation, had her pants pulled down and whacked her with a stick on her backside until she was bleeding.

Fearing an arrest by the FBI, Jones fled the country with his followers and went to Guyana. Before leaving the country, however, Jones met with his followers. He told his people that the FBI was trying to harass them, and he released a rattlesnake into the congregation. The rattlesnake slithered around the people's feet and greatly frightened them, but Jones did not tell them the venom had been taken out of the rattlesnake. He wanted the people to be aware of snakes and to be afraid of them.

Jones then instructed his followers to take the next plane to Guyana. When they got there, he told the people never to leave their compound because snakes surrounded it. Jones had picked out land that was not conducive to farming, but he had his people trying to grow crops and working up to fifteen hours a day in temperatures as high as 120 degrees. Any complainers were given drugs and punished. Despite all this, Jonestown continued to grow in numbers.

At night, his angels would fire guns outside the compound. Jones would tell the people it was the FBI shooting and that they needed to stay together. Little did Jones's followers know that when they went to Guyana, they left behind the right of protection from the FBI. One time, Jones was heard yelling at a young boy, who was being punished, as he took the boy outside the compound. Jones then tied the boy up and left him in the area believed to be full of snakes and under threat by the FBI.

Jones told his followers that he moved to Guyana because the United States was becoming a racist place to live. He told them that Guyana was a place where they could live in peace, and it was the only country in South America where English was spoken. It is interesting to see how Jones was able to control people. Obviously he was a very intelligent man and might have become a millionaire in a legitimate manner, but he chose not to.

On November 17, 1978, U.S. Congressman Leo Ryan, from the San Francisco Bay area, visited Jonestown, investigating claims of abuse within the People's Temple. Congressman Ryan had traveled to Guyana with Jacques Speier and some other people. There was only one dirt road leading into Jonestown, and Congressman Ryan was nervous because he had not received permission from Jim Jones to visit. Ryan had also been warned not to go to Jonestown, because Jones was a dangerous man and Ryan had no protection there. But when Ryan's group arrived in a dump truck at Jonestown, they were impressed with the facilities. Ryan thought the Jonestown followers appeared to be well fed and clothed, although he did not feel particularly welcome.

When he began talking to the followers, however, he found that many were too scared to talk to him; two people gave him notes saying they wanted to return with him to San Francisco when he left the next day. By the time Ryan was ready to leave, many other notes had been passed to Ryan begging him to take them back with him to San Francisco. But he did not have a big enough airplane for all those who wanted to travel with him.

It was later learned that Jones had a list of former members now considered enemies. Further, he had told his followers that if any of them ever left Jonestown, they would be killed. Jones had also conducted several suicide rehearsals with his members, prior to Ryan's visit, using Kool-Aid. When Jones spoke to Ryan later that first day, Jones appeared to be on drugs. On the next day, Jones was shown one of the notes given to Ryan and became visibly upset.

Ryan was told to leave the compound. As he left, he noticed men walking behind him holding guns. He and his companions returned to their plane, taking with them some of the defectors from the compound. But before the plane could take off, the men who had followed them appeared at the site and began firing shots at Ryan and his party. Congressman Ryan and three in his party were killed along with one defector. Jacques Speier and another member of Ryan's party were seriously injured, and the rest escaped into the jungle. The plane was also shot full of holes and was disabled.

While this was going on, Jones called an emergency meeting of his followers in Jonestown and told his followers that it was time to die. The people were given Kool-Aid with cyanide and told to drink it. Over nine hundred people took the Kool-Aid, and the babies were injected with cyanide. Three generations of people living in Jonestown were completely annihilated. Jim Jones, his angels, and the babies all died, with the exception of five people who were able to escape and one person who survived by hiding under a bed. Jones himself did not die from cyanide poisoning, but from what appeared to be a self-inflicted gunshot wound. His wife also killed herself and their children. Investigators were shocked to find hundreds of dead bodies, many of them already decomposing. The majority of the bodies were buried in a cemetery in East Oakland, California. Jim Jones's grandson was away playing on a basketball team or he would have been killed too. Later, other members of the People's Temple committed suicide after the fall of Jonestown.

After the mass suicide, I was asked to interview the pilot of Congressman Ryan's plane, who lived in Alameda, California. He told me how his plane was shot up and how the people fled into the jungle.

I was also given a lead to interview all of the followers of the People's Temple who did not die in Jonestown and who lived in the East Bay. The first few people I interviewed couldn't possibly be telling the truth,

I thought, but I soon realized they were. I couldn't believe the things people were willing to do for that man. When I went into their homes, they had blankets with Jim Jones's picture on them hanging in their windows, and they lit Jim Jones candles and various other items to ward off evil spirits. These people truly believed in Jim Jones and did whatever they were told to do. While interviewing these people, I learned just how cruel the man was to his followers.

When the FBI went through Jones's belongings in Jonestown, they found stacks of his followers' Social Security checks all wrapped up and ready to be cashed. They also found stacks of passports in lockers. Many turned over the deeds to their houses. You don't think that anything like this could happen, but when it does you begin to see how someone like Adolf Hitler could gain power.

At the end of 1978, the People's Temple declared bankruptcy and all of the assets went into receivership.

Escaped Prisoner

In August of 1979, in addition to receiving a raise to grade 13, I developed a very good informant. The informant told me of an individual, named John Butell, who was in Oakland driving a stolen Cadillac. Butell was an escaped prisoner carrying a weapon. But the question of where he had escaped from was an important one. If he was an escaped prisoner from a federal prison, his crime would be a federal violation and I could arrest him. However, if he escaped from a state or local prison, he would need to be arrested by a local police officer.

I told the local police in Oakland about the situation, and they went out to his workplace to arrest him. At the time, Butell was working on a roof. When he saw the police officers, he jumped off the roof and made a run for it. The Oakland police officers chased him down and arrested him. In his possession were stolen credit cards, which had been taken during a robbery in El Dorado County. The police seized the stolen Cadillac and put John Butell in jail. Later I found out that John Butell was wanted for robbery in El Dorado County and that a trial was underway.

Representatives of the El Dorado County courthouse contacted me and told me that I needed to come there and testify because Butell's public defender said that my informant had actually committed the armed robbery. When I did not go up to El Dorado County, I received a subpoena to attend the trial. After some negotiations, I was finally able to go to testify, but I let the defense know that there was no way I would ever identify my informant. Fortunately for me, a U.S. attorney was with me and when the judge told me that I would identify my informant or go to jail, the U.S. attorney stood up and told the judge of several decisions involving informants. The judge finally agreed, so I did not have to identify the informant. I would not have liked going to jail. Butell was later found guilty of the armed robbery and the case ended.

CHAPTER THIRTEEN

In the Service of Your Fellow Man

It was during this time period, 1978 to 1980, that I served as the second counselor in the bishopric of the First Ward in San Ramon. The bishop of this ward was Ralph J. Lauper. He was a great bishop and he loved the FBI. He would always shake people's hands and say, "Keep the faith." He would also say, "If you miss the fun in your calling, you have missed it all." Bishop Lauper liked to remind us that five percent of the people create ninety-five percent of our problems.

Toward the end of our service in the bishopric, Bishop Lauper told us that he was being released after nine and a half years as bishop. I really felt badly about him being released, but I felt that it wouldn't be a problem because Warren J. Crapse was the first counselor and would be the logical person to be the bishop. When I found out that the San Ramon First Ward was going to be divided into two separate wards, however, I began to experience a nervous feeling that I would be called to be bishop and I was.

I did not hesitate, however, to accept the position. The reason why I accepted the call so quickly this time was that when I'd been called as elder's quorum president, I said that I would have to think about it. I didn't think I could do it and be an FBI agent at the same time. After struggling for a week, I accepted the call, and after I had accepted it, I'd made a change from working bank robberies in Oakland to working foreign counterintelligence (FCI) cases in Berkeley. By working FCI cases, I wouldn't be called out all of the time to make arrests or have lineups, which had been the case when I'd worked bank robberies. Bishop Lauper was incredibly kind and generous. He always treated me as if he were my father. Bishop Lauper and his brother managed a furniture store. One day, when I came home, I found a new dining room table and chairs sitting on my front porch. On another occasion, I came home to see a $1,500 brass bed sitting on the porch. I asked Bishop Lauper why he had given us the bed, along with a dining room table and chairs, and he said that a customer had cancelled the orders and he thought we might like them.

When I was called to be bishop, I was concerned about how older people would feel about me being bishop. I was so young, and I felt so uncomfortable answering the phone saying, "Bishop Wright." That concern soon left me, although during the first six weeks that I was bishop we had six disciplinary councils and I went through tithing settlement with the ward members. During this time, I lost over 20 pounds because I was so concerned that I wouldn't make the right decisions as bishop. I had two great counselors, Sheldon Keala and Stewart Ivie. Later, when Sheldon Keala was released, I worked with another counselor named Paul Woodland. Sheldon Keala and Paul Woodland later served as bishops and Stewart Ivie served in several bishoprics.

During this time we had many great parties. We did many things together as a bishopric: going to baptisms, to the temple, and to various parties. As a result of this calling, I became very close to my counselors.

I also felt very close to the special interest members of our ward, who were older single adults. We took them to Oakland A's baseball games, the Ice Capades, plays, and other activities.

Once we put on a fireside for Steve Young, the former quarterback for the San Francisco '49ers. The fireside was held at the Inter-Stake Center in Oakland and I was asked to sit next to Steve. I was packing a weapon for his protection. Over five thousand people attended the fireside, and we never did have any problems. Steve had pictures taken with various people and also gave out pictures of himself to the people in attendance. Steve Young is a kind man who really cares about people.

In some ways it was hard being bishop, but in other ways it was a great experience, because the buck stops with you and if you need to make a decision to help people, as bishop you could do that.

I served as bishop from November of 1980 through May of 1985. That May, I tore the rotator cuff in my right shoulder while playing football. As a result, I was required to have shoulder surgery. It was not my first surgery for an injury sustained playing sports; in fact, I have had five knee surgeries during my life. Each of these surgeries was for a different athletic injury. My first surgery was for a wrestling injury in college, and then I had four more surgeries for softball, water skiing, tennis, and football. My walking was impaired before I had each of these surgeries. I will always be grateful for good doctors.

Shortly after my shoulder surgery, I was released as bishop. After they released me, the ward gave me a party and an engraved silver tray. It said, "The Wrights: For your years of service in the San Ramon Ward." They also gave me a plaque that said, "In loving gratitude for all of your service, from the members of the San Ramon First Ward." The plaque also had the inscription, "When ye are in the service of your fellow beings, ye are only in the service of your God." When I gave my father's eulogy in 1981, I used that same quote.

I loved being bishop and I loved seeing my young daughter Kimberly waving at me while I was sitting on the stand every Sunday morning. There is a price to being a bishop, though, in that it takes time away from family. During my years as a bishop, I would work over fifty hours a week as an FBI agent and over forty hours a week as bishop.

FBI agents were required to shoot at the firearms range at least six times a year. I always loved to shoot in the FBI and always felt good about my shooting record. The range for San Francisco was held at the prison in Pleasanton, which was located about two miles from my house. Agents would come from FBI offices all over northern California to shoot at this location. Since I lived so close to the range, I took advantage of the opportunity to go home for lunch.

AGENTS AT THE FIREARMS RANGE

One hot summer afternoon, I walked into my house holding my jacket, which I had taken off since it was so warm.   My five-year-old daughter, Kimberly, and her five-year-old friend were in the living room with my wife, and I did not see them as I walked past, although I heard my daughter's friend as she said, "Kimberly, your dad has on a gun."

Kim said, "Yes, it's his job. It is what he does at work." The girl then asked, "What does he do at work?"   Kim replied, "He is a bishop."

JIM & KAREN WITH THEIR FIVE CHILDREN

John Rowland's Banana Splits

As I mentioned, FBI agents like to find humor wherever they can. One agent in Oakland, named John Rowland, had an unquenchable appetite. He would bet people that he could eat certain things. One time he won a bet by eating thirteen large chocolate éclairs. On one occasion, my good friend Bob Porter told John Rowland that he didn't believe that John could eat three banana splits at Fentons. The banana splits at Fentons, it must be acknowledged, were huge, and most people could not even eat one by themselves. John declared that he could eat three banana splits, and several of us agents were eager to see if he actually could. A few of us went with Rowland at lunchtime to witness this eating spree.

Bob Porter, however, went to Fentons beforehand and talked the waitresses into making extra large banana splits for John.

We arrived at Fentons, were seated, and the waitress brought in the first banana split for John Rowland. It was enormous and even the bananas were extra big. That didn't bother John; he began eating the banana split and drinking coffee at the same time in order to melt the ice cream faster. He finished the first one and started eating the second one. It was hard to believe that he could actually finish two of these enormous banana splits, but he did. The waitresses began feeling sorry for John, and so the third banana split was not as big. John looked at the third banana split and said, "I give up." All of us had a good laugh over that, and I am sure that that as stories are retold, they only get bigger and better.

Bob Porter's Death

One year, Karen, the kids, and I took a family vacation to Montana. After the vacation, we headed back to California, and while in a motel in Idaho, I turned on the television set. The announcer said that Agent Charles W. Elmore and Agent J. Robert Porter had been shot and killed by a terrorist who was also killed in the El Centro Resident Agency. I couldn't believe what I was hearing. Bob Porter was the most capable agent I had ever known.

Bob Porter had been working as a senior resident agent in the El Centro Resident Agency after being transferred from San Francisco to San Diego. When agents examined the El Centro office and checked out the weapons and bullet holes, they determined that the terrorist had knocked on the door and Bob had opened it. The terrorist rushed in holding a shotgun. Bob grabbed the shotgun and threw the man to the floor. Bob then sat on the terrorist as he took the shotgun away from him. The other agent, seeing that Bob had things under control, put his weapon away. However, while the terrorist was lying on his back, he pulled a handgun out from his waist, which neither agent had seen, and shot both men. The terrorist was also shot in the melee, and all three men died in the El Centro office.

The same day that Charles W. Elmore and J. Robert Porter were killed, another agent named Johnnie L. Oliver was shot and killed in Cleveland, Ohio. This was something that had never happened in the FBI, having three agents die on the same day.

When I heard about Bob, I decided that it was better for me to go to El Centro than to go home. I felt that I could help Bob's wife and family and attend his funeral. I telephoned Bob's wife, Flora, and she asked me if I could come down for the funeral and be one of the pallbearers. I said yes, and we began our trip to El Centro. On our way, we traveled to Las Vegas and the car began to have problems and could not be driven any further.

I decided to leave Karen and the children at a hotel and fly to El Centro. After several delays and two different flights, I finally arrived at Bob's funeral service just before it began. I had just enough time to meet with Flora in the viewing room and then go into the service. It was amazing how many law enforcement officers dressed in full uniform were there. It was a beautiful service and the director of the FBI flew in to speak. Agent Ray Campos, who was working in San Juan, Puerto Rico, also flew in and gave the eulogy for Bob.

Bob Porter's favorite restaurant had been Fentons, the home of the famous banana split eating contest. The restaurant is located on Piedmont Avenue in Oakland and one older waitress, named Marge, particularly enjoyed taking care of the agents who faithfully came in for lunch. She especially liked Bob, so when she found out that Bob was being transferred to San Diego, she invited the agents to come in so she would treat us all to a milkshake or sundae. We tried to talk her out of it, but she was adamant that she was going to do this. We showed up at Fentons and had a great time. She was truly one of the best waitresses I have ever known. Marge then said good-bye to Bob Porter and the party ended.

Sometime after Bob Porter was killed, I went into Fentons not realizing that Marge didn't know Bob had been killed. When I sat down at the table, she came up to me and asked about Bob. I had to tell her that he had been shot and killed in El Centro. Marge immediately burst into tears, causing several customers at Fentons to look over to see what was wrong. I was sorry I had to be the one to tell her, because I knew how much she liked and admired my friend. Bob Porter was the finest agent I have ever known.

CHAPTER FOURTEEN

Twenty Years with the FBI

Striped Bass

Sometime in 1978, I went fishing in the Martinez Bay in California with former agent, Frank Burroughs, and a friend of his. Burroughs had his own fishing boat and we were using live minnows trying to catch striped bass. I caught two of the three bass, which was just a matter of luck, and then we had only one minnow left and it was dead. I couldn't decide whether to put it on the hook. I thought, what do I have to lose? I hooked the minnow on and cast my line out.

Within a few minutes, my line started sailing out. I thought the fish was going to take out all of my line before it stopped. I didn't know what was on the end of my line, but I knew that it must be big. The fish then turned and started coming toward the boat and I couldn't reel in the line fast enough. I fought the fish for several minutes and finally got it up to the boat where we could see what a large bass I had hooked. Frank then netted the fish and brought it into the boat. It was a thirty-four-pound striped bass, and I was really proud of my catch. I want everyone to know: That fish tasted delicious!

JIM WITH SEABASS

Water Rafting

Another time, some agents and I went water rafting down the American River in California. The American River can get quite rough, and I have a picture showing the six-man raft going completely under water after running into very large rapids. I never did find my hat after that event, but we were grateful to be alive. I remember another time going down the American River with my son Jimmy. We got out of the six-man boat and got into a two-man kayak. It was crazy getting into a kayak when we knew nothing about steering a kayak. We wound up being dumped out of that kayak. It was unbelievable how swift and cold that water was heading down the American River, with nothing to protect us. We were both lucky to live through that incident. The water moves so fast that while in the water, if you did not keep your legs up, they could easily be broken on the rocks.

JIM AND COMPANY GOING DOWN THE AMERICAN RIVER

East Bay Rapist

In 1978, a man began attacking women in Concord, Danville, and San Ramon. He was known as the East Bay rapist, and he had the women in San Ramon very nervous because they felt they might be next. The rapist would enter a person's house at two or three o'clock in the morning and go into the bedroom where the husband and wife were sleeping. He would shine a flashlight in the husband's eyes and show him the gun he was carrying in his other hand. He would tell the husband that if he moved he would kill him. The rapist instructed the husband to lie on his stomach and have the wife tie him up. He would take the wife into the kitchen to get dishes to pile on the back of the husband. He then would tell the husband that if he heard the dishes move, he would kill his wife and then come and kill him. He did this with each of the rapes he committed. He would then take the wife into another room, rape her, and then steal any items he wanted before he finally left.

After committing several rapes in the East Bay area, he traveled to Los Angeles and began raping women there. His DNA has been matched both in Los Angeles and the East Bay, but he has never been arrested.

While he was raping in San Ramon, my neighbors became very nervous. They knew that I was a special agent for the FBI and asked me if there was anything that I could do. I told them I could hook up a wire to their house and attach it to my house. If anyone came into their house, all they had to do was push a button and I would hurry to their home with a gun. That helped three of my neighbors feel very comfortable, although we never had to use the hook-ups.

One night in 1979, I went to bed and was sleeping soundly when Karen, who was almost asleep, heard someone walking on the deck outside our bedroom. She could hear the footsteps clearly, because in the summertime we kept the sliding glass door open for the cool night air. At first she thought that it was our daughter coming home from work, but when the person put his hands on the screen, it was obvious it was a man.

"Who are you?" my wife yelled, which woke me up. Still half asleep, I took off after the stranger, hitting the screen so hard that it flew all the way to the fence, which was twenty-five feet away. I chased the person out of our yard and down the street, but was not able to catch him. About the time he got away, I started to feel kind of strange because I was dressed only in my underwear and was glad that no one saw me.

I went back and put on my clothes, got my gun and handcuffs, then sat in my car waiting for this person to return to get to his car, which I assumed was in the area. He never came back. So I finally called the police department, which sent some officers to the house with red lights blazing and sirens blaring. They asked me where he'd gone, I told them, and added that it had been almost half an hour ago. When they asked why I had waited so long to call them, I told them I was an FBI agent and had been waiting to catch him when he returned. I also needed to get dressed. The police told me they didn't care if I was naked. They told me about a burglar who went into a house where the husband, who was completely naked, had jumped the burglar and sat on him until the police arrived. Sometimes you don't make the right decision.

Late one night, I saw smoke coming off the roof of our neighbor's house. I tried to call her several times, but she did not answer her phone. I then went down and knocked on her door, but there was no answer.

"This is Jim Wright!" I yelled as loud as I could. "Open your door!" and she opened the door. As I walked in, her husband, who was a fireman, arrived at the house and asked me what was going on. Apparently, the wife had thought I was an intruder, or possibly the East Bay rapist, and was afraid to answer the door. The smoke that seemed to be coming off the roof of her house was simply steam coming from the dryer in her home. All three of us had a good laugh over this, and thus ended my heroism. It was a good thing we had a good relationship and a good sense of humor.

Five People Kidnapped

In January of 1980, I worked a case that involved the kidnapping of five individuals. It appeared to have involved drugs and $40,000 that the kidnappers claimed had been taken from them during a robbery at the home of one of the victims. The victims were Rodney Offerman and his wife, Mary, both twenty-two years old; their child, who was eighteen months old; Karen Root, who was twenty years old; and her brother, Randy Root, who was twenty-eight years old.

Randy, who suffered from leukemia, was released after the first day. He had been beaten and was listed in grave condition after his kidnapping. Mary Offerman had a broken wrist and burns on her chest from a lit cigarette. The kidnappers had told one of Mary's relatives, "You will never see Mary alive unless the ransom is paid."

The FBI had received word that the kidnappers and their victims were staying at the Edgewater Hyatt Hotel on Hegenberger Road in Oakland. We set up stations around the kidnappers' rooms and started evacuating the other guests. We expected there might be trouble as we were told the kidnappers were armed with Uzis.

We received word that the kidnappers and their victims were leaving their rooms and coming toward us so we waited for them. When they didn't come, the other agents returned to our room.

I decided to wait in the hall just in case. The next thing I knew, three kidnappers and their victims were walking down the hall toward me. I hesitated for a moment, thinking I should draw on them but then realized I would probably be killed. So I went into the room and notified the other agents that the group had just passed me in the hall.

We followed them out of the building and into the parking lot, where we surrounded them and forced them to lay on their stomachs in the pouring rain. It was approximately three o'clock in the morning. The one person I had on the ground, in the process of handcuffing, said she was one of the victims. I told her to shut up and cuffed her, but later found out that she was, in fact, one of the victims. She and the other victims were soon released.

FBI agents and police officers from Oakland and San Leandro made the arrests. Those arrested that morning were Wayne Vincent Anderson, age thirty-three, an Oakland fireman and nephew of the Oakland mayor at the time; Ezra George Peterson, age thirty-three, of Castro Valley, who had been recently released from state prison; and Mahria Carol Jordan, age thirty-one. Seized at the time of the arrests were a sawed-off shotgun, a revolver, and a machine gun.

No ransom was paid, although some of the relatives had begun making contacts to raise the money.

Church of Hakeem

In January and February of 1980, I worked on a Ponzi scheme which involved the Church of Hakeem. Hakeem was the leader of the church and he told people that they could be rich and increase their earnings by 400 percent. Three FBI agents and I went to the Church of Hakeem; I carried a briefcase, which had a camera inside of it. We wanted to get all of the leaders' names, which were posted on the wall inside the church. I took a couple of pictures without anyone knowing what I was doing, and the pictures were later used to prosecute some people.

Hakeem was a very bright man who could have been a millionaire working legitimate concerns, but he preferred to use the pyramid scheme to make his money. The FBI received a warrant to arrest Hakeem, which we did. We took him to the FBI office in Oakland. Another agent and I interviewed Hakeem. When I would ask him a question, he would face me, and when the other agent would ask him a question, he would turn and face him. The FBI seized many items belonging to Hakeem, including his yacht.

When we first interviewed the followers of the Church of Hakeem, they did not want to talk to us because they were afraid they would lose their money. As with any pyramid scheme, however, the people who had invested first made money, and everyone else lost their money. The leaders of the Church of Hakeem were convicted of this white-collar crime.

In June of 1980, someone put poison in aspirin bottles in the Lucky store in San Leandro, California, and then demanded $19,000 or he would continue to put poison in products at the Lucky stores. The Cupertino store also had poison and garlic powder put into their aspirin bottles. I was able to work this case. All of the extortionists were arrested and convicted.

On February 2, 1981, at my request, I was transferred to the Berkeley Resident Agency from the Oakland Resident Agency. One month later, on on March 2, my father died in his sleep and I went back to New Jersey to give the eulogy at his funeral. My father and I had always been very close, and I felt it was better that he died in his sleep rather than suffer a long agonizing period, as some people do before they die.

On April 5, 1981, the floor beneath the Berkeley Resident Agency was bombed. The decision was made at that time to close that office and combine with the Oakland office, which then became known as the East Bay Metropolitan Resident Agency. On June 27, 1981, I received my ten-year FBI service pin.

In 1982, the Wright family had a reunion at the Swiss Chalet in Midway, Utah. The Swiss Chalet is at the north end of Deer Creek Reservoir, approximately forty miles from Salt Lake City. We all had a good time, and my brother Jeff and I decided we would go down the Provo River on rubber rafts. We each had our own raft, and we knew that the water got very rapid at Bridal Veil Falls. We decided that we would grab hold of a line at Bridal Veil Falls to keep from going any further down the rapid river. At first it was very easy rafting, but as we got closer to Bridal Veil Falls, it suddenly got very swift. As we went by the falls, we tried to grab hold of the line but missed it. Now we were in the very swift part of the river. Jeff's raft broke at the bottom and he hit the rocks. He was lucky that he wasn't seriously injured.

When we got down to the bottom of the Provo River, there was a man standing on the road, looking down at us and taking our pictures. We walked up to the road and asked the man why he was taking pictures of us. He answered, "Nobody in their right mind would come down the Provo River this time of year." He told us he worked for the newspaper and said our pictures would be in the paper the next day. We bought newspapers the next day and, sure enough, Jeff's picture was in the paper, but mine was omitted.

I was always grateful that I bought a house in San Ramon, California, when I did, because after that the price of houses skyrocketed. One of the agents I worked with, named Al Dougal, rented all the years he lived in the San Francisco Bay Area. We told Al on several occasions that he needed to buy a home because the price of homes would continue to rise, but he never did. Then we started to give him some real pressure. I said, "Al, you need to buy a home." At this time, Al was transferred from San Francisco to Anchorage, Alaska. He made more money and was finally able to buy a home for $136,500 in Eagle River, Alaska, after his move in 1983. During the next several years, the market dropped and Dougal's home dropped in value by $51,500. Initially, each of us who had given him advice to buy a home was sorry that we gave him that advice. However, after the market had dropped the value of his house to $85,000, the market began to rise again, and in 2003 Dougal was able to sell his house for $208,000. After Dougal made a profit of $71,500 on his house, we all felt better about our advice.

In 1986, I was called to be the Boy Scout committee chairman. I took the best people I could from the ward, and we were able to raise a lot of money for Boy Scouts of America. At the time, Sheldon Keala was the Scoutmaster.

Rex and Freda's Golden Anniversary

In March of 1986, I was able to take Karen's parents, Rex and Freda, and all of their family to a Giants baseball game at Candlestick Park in San Francisco. The Sutherlands came down to our home in San Ramon for their fiftieth wedding anniversary. I didn't tell any of them I had made arrangements with the Giants organization. During the seventh inning, they flashed on the scoreboard, "The Giants Wish a Happy Golden Anniversary to Rex and Freda." That saying stayed on the board for a half an inning and my in-laws were really excited. I took a picture of the scoreboard, and it looked as though thousands of people came out to support the Sutherlands for their golden wedding anniversary.

THE GIANTS GAME & THE SUTHERLAND'S 5OTH
ANNIVERSARY

Freda was quite an artist, painting watercolors of various settings and selling them for $150 each, although I knew I could have easily gotten her five hundred dollars in San Francisco for the same paintings. She was very generous and several of her paintings are hanging in our house.

Walker/Whitworth Espionage Case

The United States of America is a great country. We enjoy and revere the freedoms which our forefathers fought for during the Revolutionary War. However, sometimes greed and self-indulgence overshadow the perception of these freedoms. In 1987, one man cared more about himself than the freedom and safety of our country. John Anthony Walker joined the Navy in 1955 and at one time during his career was stationed aboard the nuclear- powered submarine, the USS *Andrew Jackson,* in South Carolina. He met and married Barbara Crowley. They were the typical American family—with four children, a mortgage, family vacations—just living the American Dream. But it wasn't enough. Walker started spying for the Soviet Union in 1967 because he was having financial difficulties. It was easy. He just walked into the Soviet Embassy in Washington DC, and sold a classified document for several thousand dollars. It became routine each month; he provided classified material to the Soviets and received the money he craved to satisfy his wants. Walker convinced his wife to help him and later used Jerry Whitworth, who was a radioman in the Navy. After Walker retired in 1976, he recruited his older brother Arthur and his son Michael to help him commit espionage.

He obviously had no loyalty to his country or to his wife, Barbara. He divorced her and refused to give her alimony payments. She didn't just stand by and accept her fate as the scorned woman. Barbara notified the FBI of her former husband's transgression as a traitor to his country. After the FBI conducted an investigation, John Anthony Walker, Arthur Walker, and Michael Walker were arrested. The FBI in San Francisco arrested Jerry Whitworth. Walker pled guilty and was sentenced to life in prison. He provided details of his spying and gave testimony against Jerry Whitworth in exchange for a plea with the prosecutors that his son, Michael, would not receive a sentence of more than twenty-five years. Michael Walker was released from prison in February of 2000 because he played a minor role in the case and agreed to testify against his father, his uncle, and Jerry Whitworth. Jerry Whitworth received a sentence of 365 years in prison for his involvement. Arthur Walker also received a life sentence. Because of the codes that Walker and his associates gave to the Russians, the Russians were able to monitor our naval transmissions. The John Anthony Walker/Jerry Whitworth espionage case was described by the *New York Times* as "the most damaging Soviet spy case in the history of our country."

In early 1988, I was sent to Quantico for additional training for the FBI. I loved going back to Quantico for training because it gave me the opportunity to go up to New Jersey to see my relatives. During this time, my brother Jeff was dating a girl named Kristin Rose. Kristin was a beautiful young lady, who later married my brother. I listened to Kristin singing with her band, and then the band took a break. The trumpet player in the band was a man named Dick Caton, who used to be my cross-country coach in high school. Dick came over to us and my brother told him that I was in the FBI. Another band member, Dominick, who was obviously Italian, overheard the conversation. Dominick immediately came up to me and said, "I know what FBI stands for." I asked Dominick what FBI stands for, and he said, "Forever bothering Italians."

In 1987, I was called to work in the Pleasanton Stake high council where I served for five years. As part of the high council, I was required to speak at different wards every month. I enjoyed speaking to these wards and they always treated me with respect.

I also coached the young men's softball team. I had some of the finest young athletes in the stake. These young men ranged in age from fourteen to eighteen years old. They knew how to play softball, and we had several home run hitters. As a result, we always had the best team in our stake and it was easy being the coach when we had such good athletes. The softball team won several tournaments, and I was presented with a softball signed by all the players

During this time, I also attended various in-services offered by the FBI in Quantico, Virginia, which really helped me in my training and gave me opportunities to visit my relatives in New Jersey.

On June 27, 1991, I received my twenty-year pin with the FBI. It is amazing how quickly the twenty-year period went. It was obvious that I chose the right career when I chose to be an agent for the FBI.

CHAPTER FIFTEEN

A New Enemy

Melanoma

In November of 1991, my wife, Karen, had a routine physical exam. I offered to take time off work and go with her, but she said that I didn't need to; it was just a routine examination. When I got home, my wife was in tears. I asked what the problem was and she told me that after the physical, the doctor told her she had advanced stages of melanoma and only had three months to live. I couldn't believe it.

I was so shocked by the news that I took Karen for a second opinion, which confirmed the first opinion: She only had three months to live. I attempted to find out as much as I could about how to fight the melanoma, but all I found was that there was a new treatment: interleukin. When I checked with my insurance company, they told me there wasn't any way they would pay for interleukin treatment.

I then discovered an organization called the City of Hope, whose headquarters were in southern California. The City of Hope was going through all kinds of experiments with interleukin, and I drove down there with Karen to see if she could be given the interleukin treatment. I will always remember how kind the people were at the City of Hope Hospital. The hospital treats various patients with all kinds of cancer, including melanoma.

We got a room outside the hospital and then Karen was admitted as a patient. She was there for a few weeks going through the interleukin treatments. While she was in the hospital, her femur, or thighbone, broke. I don't know what we would have done if she hadn't been in the hospital at the time.

At first, the interleukin treatment appeared to be working. Although the bill for the hospital and treatment was climbing to over $300,000, officials at the City of Hope Hospital told me there would not be any charge for Karen, and they would take care of any bills. We went home, but later returned to the hospital for additional treatment and then went home again.

I'll always remember how kind the FBI was to me and to my family when they transferred me to the Los Angeles office and I was able to work at the hospital facilities. After returning home the second time, the SAC from San Francisco transferred me to the Hayward Resident Agency so that I could work out of Hayward and still be close to home if my wife needed me.

It was a special time for my wife. Karen planned for her own funeral service, made afghans for me and for each of our children, and planned Christmas for our family. She told me that she knew that she was getting ready to die, and she wanted to talk to our son Brian, who was on a mission for the church in Bahia Blanca, Argentina. We talked to the mission president and then were able to talk to Brian. Karen told Brian that she was very proud of him, and that she was preparing to die. She told him she wanted him to stay on his mission and not return home, because he had worked very hard to learn Spanish and had come to love the Argentineans. If he came home, he would not be able to return to Argentina and would have to stay in the United States.

After his mission was completed, Brian told me how much he loved his mother, and that her decision for him to stay in Argentina had been the right one. If he had come home, he said, all he would have done would have been to cry.

The interleukin therapy did help my wife and she was able to live for twelve months, but the treatment did not save her from the melanoma. It was amazing: before she died, people would come to our home and try to cheer up Karen. What they found was that Karen would cheer them up. I am also grateful for the quilt which was given to her by friends. They quilted together seventy-four squares, representing seventy-four memories that we had of our family and friends.

I began taping my wife's life story. It was interesting that she could dictate better than I could, and I dictated all the time at work. She was able to get through most of her life and through the lives of three of her children, and then she slipped into a coma and died a couple of days later. She died in my arms at 1:45 AM on November 6, 1992. I knew the second she died that she was gone, and instead of calling the doctor or the hospital, I called the members of our family.

Although I knew her pain and suffering had been intense, and she was now free of it, the sense of loss was worse after she was gone, because we had been married for twenty-eight years and our marriage had been such a happy one.

In all my life I have never known a woman who had so much courage. Karen was so good to our children and me. I remember how she would sit in the upstairs hallway when our five children were in bed, getting ready to go to sleep, and each night she would tell them a different story. Our children loved their mother very much, as I did. She was the most courageous woman I have ever known.

Karen's funeral service was a wonderful service, which was not surprising since she had planned it.

JIM'S FIVE CHILDREN

After I was released from the stake high council in 1992, I was called in to serve as a high priest group leader in the San Ramon First Ward. I served as high priest group leader from 1992 through 1994, and then was called by the stake president to be the stake mission president in the new Danville California Stake. Our ward had just been reassigned to be in the Danville California Stake, and when I was called to be stake mission president, I told the stake president, Dean Davies, that I had never served a mission and had no idea how to be a stake mission president. He told me I would learn, and because the stake had changed and included Danville and Alamo, he recommended that I pick people from Danville and Alamo to be my two assistants. I told him I did not know anyone from Danville or Alamo, but he gave me the names of people who would make good assistants for me.

He chose one person from Danville and one from Alamo, and also chose my secretary. I felt strange about having assistants called who I didn't even know. Our first meeting took place in the stake president's high council room, and was attended by my two assistants, my secretary, and all of the missionaries from the stake. When I came into the room and sat down, I realized I did not know one person in that room, and was convinced I did not know how to be a stake mission president. Fortunately for me, my first counselor knew a lot about being a stake mission president and taught me well.

I was able to work many cases as a special agent in Oakland. In February 1994, I had a case that involved the escape of several individuals from Her Majesty's prison in England. I did a lot of surveillance work on this case and on February 23, agents from our office arrested one of the escapees.

Hell's Angels Investigation

I also became involved with an investigation of the Hell's Angels. We had search warrants issued for approximately twenty-five homes, and we decided to hit them all at the same time. One of the Hell's Angels was on a plane and we arrested him when he arrived back in Oakland. Almost all of the Hell's Angels were in the East Bay. The house that I hit with another agent was the house of the international secretary of the Hell's Angels. He was home at the time and we confiscated several articles, among them his computer records, which disclosed the Hell's Angels "street names" throughout the world. It was a great find.

While we served the search warrant at this house, agents served another search warrant for a house down the street. While searching the home, they heard noises in the garage. They opened the door slightly, stuck shotguns through the opening, and turned on the light. What they saw were two chickens running around the garage.

The agents took all of their evidence and put it in a three-by-five-foot box. They also put the two chickens in the box and then covered it with a heavy burlap blanket. When one of the other agents came in and asked to see the evidence, they said sure. When he lifted the burlap blanket, the two chickens jumped out at him. The agents then decided to have some fun. They knew that a car used by a couple of agents was parked nearby. We knew how to open the car door without a key, so we threw the two chickens in there and then locked the car back up again. When the agents jumped into their car, were they surprised! The chickens were all over them. Sometimes you just have to have fun when you work for the FBI.

Meth Lab

An ex-felon was living in a home in the county north of San Francisco, up highway 101 in the city of Willits. The owner of the home had two pit bulls, which he kept outside. As FBI agents surrounded the house early in the morning, one of the pit bulls ran down the driveway toward one of the agents, who shot and killed the dog. Even though the agent had a silencer on his gun, the gun still made a clicking noise.

The owner heard the clicking noise and immediately called the county sheriff's office. When an agent attempted to call the owner after the other agents had surrounded the house, the man's phone line was busy. The agent had the operator cut in on the line and found out that the owner had called the county sheriff's office to report that unknown individuals had just shot his dog outside his house. The agents told him to surrender, and he was arrested without incident.

When the agent who was covering the back of the house realized the ex-felon had been arrested, he took the bolt out of his rifle and walked toward the house. Unbeknownst to him, the second pit bull was in the backyard watching him. When the agent saw the pit bull, he knew that he had taken the bolt out of his rifle and didn't know whether he had enough time to grab his pistol. This second pit bull, however, was a lot smarter than the first one. He saw the agent's gun and ran and hid under an SUV, where he remained for a very long time.

The evidence removed from the house included a complete meth lab. The agents also removed several weapons, which the ex-felon knew he could not legally own.

Knee Surgery

Later in 1994, I had my fifth and final knee surgery. As mentioned earlier, I have had five knee surgeries, each surgery for a different athletic injury. All of my doctors have been very good and this doctor was equally outstanding.

Prior to the surgery, I had a good conversation with the anesthesiologist, and we quickly became friends. He asked me whether there was anything he could do to help me, and I told him that I would be interested in having a film of my surgery. The surgery was a new procedure in which incisions were not needed. Two holes were poked in the knee, then cartilage was taken out. Normally, the patient is walking the next day.

When I woke up in the recovery room after the surgery, there was a film sitting on my bed next to me. While recovering at home, I put the film on the TV. It showed the surgery and also played the conversation that the doctors had during the surgery. During the surgery, one of the doctors said, "Operating on his knee is like rearranging deck chairs aboard the Titanic."

Later, during a visit to the doctor, I talked to the head surgeon and said, "I wonder which doctor said that they were rearranging deck chairs aboard the Titanic, when you operated on my knee." He said, "Just a minute, I want the assistant surgeon to come in here." He brought in the assistant surgeon and asked me to repeat the question. As I repeated my question, the assistant surgeon stared down at the floor. I felt sorry for him at the time and wished I had not said anything to the head surgeon. On my last visit to the hospital, the assistant surgeon told me the hospital had changed the regulations and would no longer be recording conversations between doctors during surgeries. I guess that they were concerned about being sued but, of course, I never would have sued them. I was just happy to have a successful operation.

Raising Bees

When I played shortstop for the FBI, agent Fred Fiedler was our pitcher. Fred had a great house with a swimming pool in the backyard. One day he was talking with Al Dougal, another agent, who raised bees. Al talked Fred into raising bees in his neighborhood as well. Fred set the bees in a hive in his backyard and the bees would occasionally swarm. One day he came into the office in Oakland with a large swelling about the size of a golf ball on his neck. When we asked him what happened, he said he was allergic to bees, and the bees had swarmed and he got stung on his neck. The bees had attacked his dog as well. The dog had tried to bite them and they stung him on his tongue and his throat. Fred had to take his dog to the veterinarian and got a sizable bill, but he lived through the incident.

On another occasion, Fred's bees swarmed and landed on his next-door neighbor's wooden fence. Fred was in the process of going over to tell his neighbor that the bees were his, when he saw his neighbor take a blowtorch and attack his bees. During the process, the fence caught on fire. So Fred decided not to tell his neighbor the bees were his.

When Fred came to visit me in the hospital during my last knee surgery, he gave me a small jar of honey. I told him it was very generous of him and he said, "Oh, no, it was just a small jar." I told him it probably cost him several hundred dollars.

CHAPTER SIXTEEN

Transfer to Salt Lake City

In 1995, I requested a transfer from San Francisco to Salt Lake City. I knew that I was getting close to retirement and I wanted to retire in Utah. I had gone to school at Brigham Young University in Provo and I liked living there.

My best friend, Stew Ivie, had moved from San Ramon to Springville, Utah, in 1992. In the latter part of 1993, Stew had called me from his home in Springville. He told me that there was a lot for sale next to his home at a very reasonable price and wondered if I would be interested. Stew was a very close friend of mine and I trusted what he had to say. When I asked him who was selling the lot, he said the person was sitting right next to him. Without even looking at the property, I agreed to pay $31,500 for the property and Stew's neighbor agreed to sell it to me. Today you cannot buy even a smaller piece of property in Springville for anything under $200,000.

I called the SAC in Salt Lake City in September 1995, and he told me that there was no way I could get a transfer from San Francisco to Salt Lake City at this time. So I decided to retire in December 1995, and I started to build my new home in Springville, where I used to live when I was going to college. I found a good builder and some good plans. I made several changes in the plans and started building my home. At the time, I was still living in San Ramon.

I then received a telephone call from the transfer unit of the Bureau in Washington DC. They informed me that I was third on the office of preference list to go to Salt Lake City and the first two people were unable to accept the position. They asked me if I wanted to be transferred to Salt Lake City, and I immediately responded that I did. I received my orders to Salt Lake City by teletype. I was anxious to make the move since I had been having my house built.

I then received a telephone call from the assistant special agent in charge (ASAC) in Salt Lake City who congratulated me on my transfer, and told me that I would be assigned a resident agency on the Canadian border, and that I would work Indian matters there. I told him I would not be going to the Canadian border as I was building my home in Springville, and if I did not get my transfer to Salt Lake City as was promised to me, I would not be coming. The ASAC said that he was sorry and would call me back.

He did call me back and said that the special agent in charge (SAC) was adamant that I would either go to the resident agency on the Canadian border, or I would not be coming to Salt Lake City. I asked the ASAC if he thought being sent to the Canadian border was the office of preference I had been given and he said he did not. However, he said the SAC was adamant about it, and I would have to go to the resident agency on the Canadian border. I told the ASAC I would not be coming and then called the transfer unit in Washington. The transfer unit told me the SAC in Salt Lake City was within his right to assign me to the resident agency on the Canadian border, but if I did not go to Salt Lake City the SAC would lose one body because he was not going to assign anyone else to Salt Lake City this year.

Fortunately, SACs like to have as many people as possible working for them. About a week later, I received another call from the ASAC who told me that the SAC had a change of heart and I would be assigned to Salt Lake City. I told him I would be be happy to come. When I got to Salt Lake City, the SAC welcomed me and did not seem to be upset with me.

I arrived in Salt Lake City in December of 1995. The house I was building in Springville was completed the day before I arrived. Boyd Nuttle was the builder. He is known for his ability to build beautiful homes. As a matter of fact, when you see Nuttle homes you can tell who built them just by the way they look. It is wonderful to have a builder like Boyd, who takes pride in everything he does. After I moved into the home, Boyd had a settlement with me and told me that he'd charged me $1,100 for the additions in my home, which I had agreed to. He then told me he wasn't going to charge me the $1,100 and gave me the money back.

My new home was on a large piece of property and I purchased enough Kentucky bluegrass to sod it all. I wasn't expecting more than five people to come to help me sod my home, but to my delight twenty-eight people from the neighborhood showed up to do the work. We were able to lay all of the sod in less than two hours, which was truly unbelievable.

In 1995, I requested my personnel record from the FBI. I was surprised at how easy it was to obtain this information. They sent me everything and I am proud of the fact there was not one negative entry made in my personnel file.

The UNABOM Case

Sixteen Innocent Victims

Prior to being transferred to Salt Lake City, I had been working many hours as a member of the UNABOM Task Force (UTF) in the San Francisco Bay Area, attempting to identify the person responsible for placing or sending fourteen bombs over a period of sixteen years.

The Unabomber was later identified as Theodore Kaczynski, a former assistant professor at the University of California at Berkeley. After two years as an assistant, Kaczynski resigned from his position. In approximately 1971, Kaczynski moved into a cabin which he had built himself near Lincoln, Montana. The cabin had no running water or electricity.

In 1978, the Unabomber's first bomb was addressed to Professor E. J. Smith at the Rensselaer Polytechnic Institute in Troy, New York. The package was never mailed. It was found in a parking lot on the Circle Campus of the University of Illinois in downtown Chicago. The finder of the package, hoping for a reward, contacted Professor Buckley Crist, who was listed as the return address. Crist knew nothing about the package and when he took the wrapping paper off the outside, he became suspicious and requested that a police officer open it. When the officer opened it, the package exploded and the officer received minor injuries.

About one year later, the Unabomber's second bomb was placed in a graduate student carousel area of the Technological Institute at Northwestern University in Evanston, Illinois. A curious graduate student opened the package and was injured.

The third bomb was sent by mail to an address in Washington DC. It detonated in a mail pod in the cargo area of American Airlines flight 444. The device functioned as it was designed, but was not properly contained; therefore, upon detonation it merely burned in the mail pod. The resulting fire caused smoke to enter the passenger compartment and cockpit of the airplane. The pilot elected to make an emergency landing when the crew could not discern the origin of the smoke. Several passengers were injured as they evacuated the airplane. The fire resulting from the detonation was within minutes of burning into the plane's main hydraulic support system. Had that occurred, the seventy-five passengers and crew would certainly have perished in the resulting crash.

After the first three bombs, the FBI laboratory learned of the first two devices. They obtained the evidence from those incidents and compared them with the remains of the bomb on flight 444. The FBI laboratory determined that the same individual had made all three devices.

The next bomb was sent to the CEO of United Airlines, at his residence near Chicago. The bomb delivery was preceded by a letter. The bomb, contained in a book, detonated and severely injured the CEO. Over the next eight years, the Unabomber placed or sent eight more devices, each more sophisticated in design and construction than the previous one.

Bomb number five was placed in the business classroom building on the campus of the University of Utah in Salt Lake City. It failed to detonate and was rendered safe after a student picked it up.

Bomb number six was mailed to a professor at Vanderbilt University in Nashville, Tennessee. The professor's secretary opened the mailed package and was severely injured.

Sometime after bomb number six, the FBI declared this case to be a major case and gave it the acronym, UNABOM. Previously, the bomber had been called the "The Junkyard Bomber" by law enforcement. The UNABOM acronym was chosen because universities (UN) and the airline industry (A) were the targets of the early bombs (BOM). The press then began to refer to the bomber as the UNABOMBER.

In July of 1982, the Unabomber placed the first of two devices on the campus of the University of California in Berkeley. This device exploded in a staff break room and injured a professor. Three years later, in 1985, the Unabomber placed a second device in Corey Hall. This bomb was placed in a graduate student room. A graduate student who was an Air Force Academy graduate and was now in the astronaut program opened the device, which exploded. As a result of the explosion, the student lost four fingers on one of his hands, which ended his participation in the astronaut program and his career as an Air Force pilot.

Three more bombs were sent during 1985. The next one was sent to the Fabrication Division of Boeing Aircraft in Auburn, Washington. This bomb failed to detonate and was rendered safe by a local bomb squad. The next was sent to a professor at the University of Michigan in Ann Arbor. A graduate assistant to the professor opened the device and was injured. The final bomb of 1985 was placed outside the back door of a Sacramento, California, computer store. The owner found the device, attempted to pick it up and became the first fatality of the Unabomber.

In February of 1987, the Unabomber placed a device, identical to the Sacramento bomb behind a small computer store in Salt Lake City. One of the owners of the store saw the device and attempted to pick it up. The device exploded, severely injuring him.

For the first time, however, the Unabomber had been seen by one of the employees of the store. A task force was quickly formed, but the resulting investigation failed to locate or identify the Unabomber. No more devices were mailed or placed for the next six years.

The UNABOM Task Force, on which I worked in San Francisco,

was formed in July of 1993. Attorney General Janet Reno ordered its formation, following the receipt of two bombs and a letter to the *New York Times.*

The first bomb was received in the mail by a University of California genetics professor at his Tiburon residence. The bomb exploded and severely injured him. The second bomb was mailed to the office of a Yale University computer professor in New Haven, Connecticut. When the professor opened the package, he was also injured. Shortly after these two bombs were received, an editor at the *New York Times* received a letter from the Unabomber. In this letter, the Unabomber took credit for the two most recent bombs, referred the recipient to the FBI for authenticity, and provided the editor with a "secret number" by which future communication could be authenticated.

In October of 1993, a one million dollar reward was offered when FBI Director Louis J. Freeh, the Alcohol Tobacco and Firearms (ATF) Director, and the Postmaster General held a national press conference and announced the reward to anyone who would provide information leading to the capture of the Unabomber.

The Bureau received 55,000 calls from those seeking the reward. The Unabomber case was the largest case in the history of the Bureau; the bombs sent by the Unabomber killed three people and injured twenty-three others. There were 54,000 volumes written on this case, and there were over 2,400 suspects. Each of the previous bombs was re-investigated, all of the previously gathered crime scene evidence was re-examined with new technology, and all the previous bombsites were revisited and reevaluated. Every crime laboratory in the world was contacted and asked to provide assistance. Airline records were obtained and evaluated, as were the records of all the universities involved. FAA records were obtained and examined. The task force undertook numerous special projects. The FBI Behavioral Science Unit developed new profiles. The task force sought and received the assistance of the media, and numerous programs featuring the Unabomber were aired. All of this investigating failed to identify the person responsible for placing and sending the fourteen bombs.

In December of 1994, a New York advertising executive received a package in the mail at his North Caldwell, New Jersey, residence. He was killed almost instantly upon opening the package.

The UNABOM Task Force was once more given additional resources and manpower and continued to investigate.

In April of 1995, a package was received at the Sacramento headquarters of the California Forestry Association. The package was addressed to the previous director of the Timber Association of California, a lobby group for the timber industry. The organization had recently changed its name and a new director had taken over. When the new director opened this package, he was killed almost instantly.

In June of 1995, the *New York Times* and the *Washington Post,* as well as several other entities and individuals, received a copy of a lengthy document from the Unabomber. This document became known as the "UNABOM Manifesto." In return for publishing this document, the Unabomber promised to cease killing people.

The task force made the decision to publish the "Manifesto" as a means of possibly identifying the Unabomber. It was published in its entirety by the *Washington Post* on September 19, 1995. Leads continued to pour into the task force, but none identified the Unabomber.

At the insistence of his wife, David Kaczynski, the brother of Theodore Kaczynski, read the Manifesto and recognized much of it as ideas that had been professed to him by his brother Ted. David also recognized several phrases and spellings as being unique to his brother.

For the next several months, David and his wife struggled with what to do with their suspicions. They attempted to discount Ted as a suspect by having a friend conduct an investigation. They had a linguistic comparison and an analysis done of the Manifesto as compared with other writings of Ted. But their investigation could not eliminate Ted as a suspect.

Finally in January of 1996, through a Washington, DC, attorney, the Kaczynskis came to the FBI with their suspicions. The attorney provided the FBI with enough information that the task force believed they now had the identity of the Unabomber.

The FBI had put in more time on this case than any previous FBI investigation. Some of the work included investigating the following:

(1) Various suspects

(2) Each incident

(3) Special projects

(4) Metal shops

(5) Bombing parts

(6) Various names

(7) Areas where each incident took place

(8) Every crime lab in the world

(9) Linguistics comparison

(10) Various airlines (FAA records)

(11) Academic associations

I was given the assignment to check out several metal shops in the San Francisco area. I tried to find any leads that would suggest that someone had been buying or using a particular kind of metal used in the making of bombs. Of course, it always led to a dead end. Theodore Kaczynski was not in our area at all, but we had to check out every possibility.

A small contingent of FBI agents was sent to rural Montana, the area in which Theodore Kaczynski lived. These agents were also tasked with insuring that Kaczynski did not leave his Montana cabin to mail any additional bombs.

Another group of FBI agents was dispatched to interview and work with David Kaczynski, his wife, and his mother in an effort to develop additional probable cause for the affidavit for the application of the search warrant for Kaczynski's Montana residence.

On April 3, 1996, two FBI agents, UTF Supervisor Max Noel and Helena, Montana, Senior Resident Agent Tom McDaniel, and a U.S. Forest Service police officer approached Kaczynski's rural cabin near Lincoln. Using a ruse, they enticed Kaczynski out of his cabin, detained him, and served the federal search warrant. The subsequent search yielded the following evidence:

(1) Notebooks (ten thousand pages)

(2) Switches

(3) Codes

(4) A fully functional bomb ready to be mailed

(5) The formula for making explosives

(6) Various escape routes

(7) Forty-four thousand pages of notes

(8) The original of the Manifesto

(9) The antique typewriter used to type the Manifesto and other UNABOM letters and other documents.

Kaczynski's principle method of transportation in and around the Lincoln area had been a bicycle. When traveling to other areas of the country to mail and place the bombs, Kaczynski would travel by bus. He would use his proper name while staying at different hotels. Kaczynski avowed that he was glad he had killed people, and a court-appointed psychiatrist later diagnosed him as being a "paranoid schizophrenic."

David Kaczynski received the one million dollar reward for his assistance in identifying his brother as the Unabomber. After paying the IRS, he used the proceeds to pay his attorney fees and to pay for his and his mother's travel expenses to Sacramento where they attended Theodore Kaczynski's legal proceedings. With the money that remained, David established a fund for the victims of violent crime.

In early 1998, after lengthy proceedings in the federal district court in Sacramento, Kaczynski agreed to plead guilty to all of the government's charges. He did this in order not to be portrayed at the trial as a mentally ill individual. His attorneys planned to use a "diminished capacity defense" during the sentencing phase of the trial. Kaczynski could not bear to be portrayed in that fashion.

In May of 1998, Theodore J. Kaczynski was sentenced to four consecutive life sentences by Federal District Judge Burrell, who noted at the sentencing that Kaczynski showed utterly no remorse for his unspeakable and monstrous crimes. Kaczynski is serving his sentence at the federal government's "super-max" penitentiary at Florence, Colorado.

Most of this information about the Unabomber was provided by a friend of mine, Max Noel, who was the co-case agent in this investigation and one of the three FBI supervisors in the Theodore Kaczynski case.

CHAPTER SEVENTEEN

Justice Township

Montana Freemen Case

If I had thought that all of the great cases were in the San Francisco area, I soon found out I was mistaken. One of the biggest cases to come along while I was working in the Salt Lake City FBI office involved the Montana Freemen.

The Salt Lake City office has jurisdiction over Utah, Idaho, and Montana, where the Freemen were located. They were a group of men and women who banded together with the common belief that they were superior to all others. They claimed to be Christians and believed that God considered white people to be the superior race. It certainly sounded as if they had taken their beliefs right out of the pages of Adolf Hitler's book and from Nazi Germany.

These Freemen moved onto a sheep ranch surrounded by a wheat field in Jordan, Montana. They did not acknowledge any federal, state, or county governments. They claimed to be an entity unto themselves.

They were quietly contacting and training people from all over the United States to increase their following.

The leader of the group was LeRoy Schweitzer. His right-hand man was Daniel Peterson Jr. They often traveled around the country giving seminars to people with their same beliefs, and some of their followers would travel to Jordan to be trained. They taught their followers fraudulent schemes intended to destroy the banking system in the United States. They issued bad checks to buy cars, homes, personal items, and to support their cause. They intimidated public officials and filed liens against them, supposedly because the elected officials violated their oaths of office. They then sold the liens to generate money for their organization. They also acquired guns and ammunition to protect themselves.

When the group first moved to Jordan, the townspeople were happy to have them there, but soon found that the Freemen did not want to abide by the laws of the town. The Freemen refused to pay any kind of taxes, register their cars, or recognize any authority in Jordan whatsoever. They referred to their compound as "Justice Township" and themselves as the "Freemen," meaning they were free from any government other than their own.

The FBI was brought in to investigate when it was discovered the Freemen were committing crimes. There were many agents from the Salt Lake City office who worked a lot of hours on this case. The first phase of the investigation included gathering information on the Freemen. It took us several months before we could gather enough information to make arrests.

My first assignment was in Billings, Montana. The FBI obtained a court order for wiretaps on the Freemen's phones. I would go to Billings, Montana, for two weeks at a time and work twelve-hour shifts. The shifts consisted mostly of listening to conversations from phones inside the Freemen's headquarters. We would spend hours listening, summarizing, and typing up conversations. The Freemen would answer their phones by, instead of just saying hello, saying, "Justice Township." At times it seemed to be mundane work, but it was exciting when we actually got information to use in court against these lawless people. There were usually six to eight men and women on each shift.

Our investigation began in the winter and the weather in Montana was bitterly cold, often forty degrees below zero. It was so cold we had to plug our cars into engine block heaters so that we could start them when needed. One agent walked four blocks from his motel to the FBI phone tap center, and when he arrived, he could not open his eyes because his eyelashes were frozen together.

After obtaining enough evidence against the Freemen, the next phase took us to Jordan. We stayed in Miles City and drove to Jordan each day. Our work schedule was about the same as before. We were there for two weeks at a time working twelve-hour shifts. The cold winter weather stayed and it often remained forty below. The road from Miles City to Jordan was an incredible drive. It took us about an hour and we saw hundreds of antelope, deer, and Canadian geese. One day as I was driving to Jordan, I nearly struck some deer in the road. We then came upon a highway patrol car stuck on the side of the road in a ditch. The officer had swerved to miss hitting some deer in the road. I walked to a farmhouse close by and enlisted the help of the farmer. He brought his tractor and pulled the patrol car right out. He was a friendly man who was more than willing to help. I think that is the way of life for most of the people living in that area. We often see both sides of the spectrum, men fighting against men and good men willing to help others.

The FBI set up a command post in a building close by the Freemen compound. We surrounded their compound with agents armed with weapons. We watched every back road and had every inch of the place covered. There was no way any of the Freemen could escape. By using force, we could have ended the siege in a day. However, the FBI was greatly concerned about anyone getting hurt. We certainly did not want another "Ruby Ridge" on our hands.

The command post was used for several things. We attended meetings, ate meals, and received our assignments there each day. The assistant special agent in charge (ASAC) was there, and officials from Washington, DC came in at various times during the siege.

Our duties usually required us to cover the perimeter of the compound or sit in our cars guarding the road and the entrances. The media was ever-present. They had listening devices and tried to monitor our conversations. One day, another agent and I were sitting in our car guarding the gate into the FBI command post. A woman from the Freemen compound came out and was immediately taken to the post to be interviewed. The media jumped on that in a hurry and a reporter from Salt Lake City came up to us, demanding we let her into the command post to interview the woman. I told her no and she emphatically requested to see the person in charge. I told her I was in charge and that she could not go into the command post. She tromped away very angry. I was told not to let anyone in and I was going to do as I was told.

Because it was so cold, I was constantly drinking hot chocolate to keep warm. I had had kidney stones in the past, and I forgot that my doctor had told me chocolate was one of the causes of my kidney stones. Well, sure enough, it all caught up with me. I developed a kidney stone. With the excruciating pain in my back, I knew I was in trouble. I had my partner take me to the hospital in Miles City where I spent two days until I passed that stone. Of course, after passing the stone, all was well and I was back on the job.

The siege at Jordan lasted eighty-one days. The Freemen were well stocked with food and supplies and were determined to hold out. The water and electricity to their compound was disconnected. It is interesting that, all during this time, we had an undercover agent by the name of Tim Healy, who had infiltrated the Freemen group. He was inside the compound. Agent Healy set up a device to provide a security system for the Freemen compound. The security system consisted of a series of cameras and solar panels. He had the Freemen convinced that the system was very high tech, when, in fact, it didn't work at all.

Agent Healy wanted to show Schweitzer and Peterson the security system placed around the compound. One day he drove them out to see it. Of course it was all a ruse, and they were immediately surrounded by FBI agents and arrested. After the two leaders were apprehended, everyone else in the Freemen compound surrendered without a shot being fired. There were approximately twenty men, women, and children in the compound.

After several months of work on the Freemen case and hours spent wandering around in the snow and cold, I missed all of the fun because I was not in Jordan when the arrests were made. But one of the great rewards of being in the FBI is seeing justice done and dangerous people put away from harming good people in society.

The trials were held in Billings. LeRoy Schweitzer and Daniel Peterson Jr. were charged with bank and mail fraud, illegal possession of guns, threatening a federal judge, and armed robbery. They still refused to recognize the authority of the United States government. As they were brought into the courtroom to stand trial, they began yelling and disrupting the proceedings. The trial had to be resumed without Schweitzer and Peterson in the courtroom. Instead, they watched the proceedings via closed-circuit TV from their cell.

Other members of the Freemen group were also brought to trial at different times, some with lesser charges. Agent Healy, the undercover agent, provided an exhaustive testimony which lasted a day and a half. LeRoy Schweitzer and Daniel Peterson Jr. showed their contempt and hatred toward Healy. They had thought he was a trusted associate. Healy's work on this case, as an undercover agent, was a courageous act for this country. In May of 2009, Healy was promoted to Director of the FBI Terrorist Screening Center

U.S. District Judge John Coughenour was in charge of the trial. He stated, "What we are talking about is a calculated and organized program to undermine the banking system of this country and to encourage other, more ignorant people to violate the law." The losses incurred from the actions of the Freemen actually were several billion dollars. Judge Coughenour sentenced LeRoy Schweitzer to twenty-two and a half years in prison, and Daniel Peterson Jr. received a sentence of fifteen years. Justice was served.

In October of 1996, I received a letter from FBI Director Louis J. Freeh telling me that he was pleased to learn of the fine assistance I rendered in connection with this matter and it was with considerable pride that he commended me. He also advised me that over the course of this complex and extensive investigation, the Bureau's focus and resolve was sustained by the contributions of capable professionals, such as myself and many other steadfast men and women of the FBI. He also stated that as a result of the dedication and unselfish support I had rendered, a positive resolution to this high-profile matter was made possible, which once again distinguished the FBI as a premier law enforcement agency. He then offered me thanks for my tireless assistance in this regard. On June 27, 1996, Director Louis J. Freeh presented me with my twenty-five-year plaque in the Salt Lake City FBI office.

JIM WITH SALT LAKE CITY SAC & DIRECTOR
LOUIS J. FREEH

JIM WITH FBI DIRECTOR LOUIS J. FREEH

Retirement As a Special Agent

I was called to serve as an assistant in the high priest group, which I did from 1996 to 1997. I was released from this position and was then called to be the high priest group leader, where I served from 1997 to 1999 in the Hobble Creek Ninth Ward in Springville.

One of the cases I worked while in Salt Lake City took place in a small town in southern Utah. I was given an older car to help on surveillance and I was able to get as far as Beaver, Utah, when the transmission went out. I immediately got on the phone to the Salt Lake office and told them they could either send someone down for me or they would do without me working the case. The next thing I knew, they told me a plane would be sent to Beaver—there was a small airport there—and to look for the plane. As the small plane taxied down the runway, I realized the pilot was a friend of mine who I had known very well in San Ramon. His name was Bob Lund. When we took off, Bob showed me different places in southern Utah, such as Lake Powell. It is amazing how beautiful Lake Powell looks when you are looking at it from an airplane.

The FBI was able to get me another car, I was able to complete the surveillance, and we made the case. After the case was over, another pilot said he would fly me back to Salt Lake City. On the way back, he told me he wanted me to fly the plane. I told him I didn't know how to fly a plane. He said it is very easy then he shifted the control over to me and I was actually flying the plane. It was amazing that I felt so comfortable. I asked the pilot how he felt about taking me to Provo, which was five miles from my home, instead of to Salt Lake City. He told me that was fine and then asked me to land the airplane. I refused to do so, and he told me I would have to because he was not going to take control of this plane. I put my hands up in the air and said then we're going to crash. He took over and we landed in Provo. As he was leaving, he shifted the wings of the airplane back and forth in the air to wave good-bye and off he went.

I was quite fortunate to work as a special agent for the FBI from June 27, 1971, to January 1, 1997. I worked under the following directors: J. Edgar Hoover (6/27/71–5/2/72), L. Patrick Gray (5/3/72–4/27/73), William D. Ruckelshaus (4/30/73–7/9/73), Clarence Kelley (7/9/73– 2/15/78), William Webster (2/23/78– 5/25/87), John E. Otto (5/26/87–11/2/87), William Sessions (11/2/87–7/19/93), and Louis J. Freeh (9/1/93–1/1/97). I also served under two outstanding special agents in charge (SACs): Charles Weeks, of the New Haven, Connecticut office, and Richard (Dick) Held, of the San Francisco office.

I was able to interview or associate with numerous individuals including bank managers, CEOs, congressmen, senators, attorneys general, directors of the FBI, mayors, U.S. attorneys, judges, sports figures, such as Steve Young, the 49ers quarterback, presidential candidates, such as Mitt Romney, and many other people.

JIM WITH U.S. ATTORNEY GENERAL EDWARD MEESE

JIM WITH SPECIAL AGENT IN CHARGE RICHARD (DICK) HELD
– SAN FRANCISCO

JIM WITH FBI DIRECTOR WILLIAM SESSIONS

I was required to only work one year to pay back my transfer to Salt Lake City and I worked thirteen months. In January of 1997, I retired as a special agent for the Federal Bureau of Investigation. Prior to retiring, the Bureau asked me if I would consider being a special investigator for the FBI after retirement. Special investigators do not have to go into the office to work; all assignments are sent by FedEx to their homes. I was told I would have to go out and interview people, but I could dictate the investigation on a cassette and FedEx that to them. The pay was good, and I would still get my retirement from the FBI, which is a very good retirement. It sounded too good to be true, but it has worked out very well and has helped me to go on many cruises with my new wife, Sharon. I started doing background investigations for the FBI and then received credentials to work for the Defense Security Service, the National Security Agency, the U.S. Office of Personnel Management, and the U.S. Customs Service. I was so busy working these cases that I wondered why I retired at all.

After a couple of years, I decided it was too much work. I sent the credentials back to the other government agencies, and ever since, I have only been working as a special investigator for the FBI.

CHAPTER EIGHTEEN

A New Beginning

Marriage

In 2002, I began dating several different women, inasmuch as I was interested in remarrying. I enjoyed the dates and the good women I met, but I couldn't find anyone who had the qualities of my wife Karen. Then a chance encounter in Nauvoo, Illinois, of all places, changed that.

My neighbor Karen Owen met a woman by the name of Sharon Ann Ferguson Cardon on a tour in Nauvoo. Karen told Sharon that she knew a really nice, single man who lived down the street from her. She asked Sharon if she was interested in dating him, and Sharon immediately told her no. Sharon's daughter, Kassie, spoke up and said, "Mother, tell her yes." Sharon relented and we had our first date on July, 13, 2002.

On our first date, I took Sharon to dinner at Thanksgiving Point and then to a play at the outdoor SCERA Theatre in Orem, Utah. On our second date, I took Sharon to a famous restaurant in Sandy, Utah, and after we ordered, Sharon told me that she was not interested in ever getting married again. By our fourth date, however, Sharon began to change her mind.

I consider myself very lucky to have found Sharon. She is wonderful and she works hard. She likes being married to me, and I like being married to her. Although some people may not believe this, we have never had an argument and I love how she is as a person. To find two women like Karen and Sharon in one man's lifetime is truly a gift.

JIM AND SHARON

We were married on March 15, 2003, in the Mount Timpanogos Temple, then went on a twenty-two day honeymoon. My brother Jeff told me we should never go on a twenty-two day honeymoon, because it would end with us getting a divorce. But I did not believe him and our honeymoon was one of the most wonderful times I ever experienced. We started in the presidential suite in the Marriot Hotel in Provo, and then went to Reno and Virginia City, both in Nevada. We then spent a week in San Francisco, seeing many attractions including Golden Gate Park, Alcatraz, Pier 39, Scoma's Restaurant, Chinatown, the Golden Gate Bridge, Ghirardelli Square, and many other unforgettable places. Then on to Sausalito, Muir Woods, Stinson Beach, Monterey, Pebble Beach, Hearst Castle, Universal Studios, and Hollywood. After that we went to San Diego and stayed in Coronado. We watched the Padres baseball team play, and went to Seaport Village, Old Town, and the Wild Animal Park. We traveled to Las Vegas and saw all of the lights and attractions there.

Sharon's daughter, Kassie, worked for the Marriot Hotel in Provo and she helped me to get reservations at Marriot hotels and their affiliates everywhere we stayed. They were great accommodations. The last few days of our honeymoon were spent in St. George, Utah, and Bryce and Zion National Parks. In Zion National Park, we stayed in a bed and breakfast; the honeymoon suite was over twelve hundred square feet. Both Sharon and I wished we had another two weeks because it was so much fun. The Pacific Ocean was breathtakingly beautiful as we traveled down the coast of California. It was fun walking over the Golden Gate Bridge. Sharon had never been to northern California and was awed by the beautiful countryside and fun things to see and do.

From 2000 to 2003, I served as a veil worker in the Provo Temple, the ward temple preparation instructor, and ward Sunday school president. In January of 2003, I was called to the high council of the Brigham Young University 21st Stake, where I served until January of 2006. During this time, Sharon and I were called to be the Young Single Adult leaders from our ward. In 2007, I was called to be a primary teacher in the Hobble Creek Ninth Ward teaching ten-year olds, where we currently attend church. I was also called to be an ordinance worker in the Provo Temple in 2006, and I am still serving in this assignment. Sharon was also called to be an ordinance worker in the Provo Temple in June of 2003. We have been working in the temple ever since and love working together.

Vacations

Sharon and I have been to many wonderful places together. In the past six years, we have been on six different cruises. In February of 2005, we went on a Caribbean cruise to San Juan, Puerto Rico, Aruba, Curacao, St. Maarten, St. Thomas, and St. Johns. In April 2006, we went on another Caribbean cruise. We saw Fort Lauderdale and Disney World, and swam with the dolphins in Mexico. In March of 2007, we went on a Hawaiian cruise to several of the islands. In October 2007, we went on a cruise to the Mexican Riviera towns of Mazatlan, Puerto Vallarta, and Cabo San Lucas. In May of 2008, we went on another Caribbean cruise to Labadee, Haiti, Montego Bay in Jamaica, Cozumel in Mexico, and Grand Cayman. We got to see the Mayan ruins in Mexico, which was an awesome experience. Our favorite cruise line is Royal Caribbean. In March 2009, we went on another cruise to the Caribbean, this time to Puerto Rico, St. Thomas, St Maarten, and Labadee.

CRUISE SHIP

In May of 2003, Sharon and I went to Woodbury, New Jersey, and saw the sights in Amish country in Pennsylvania, New York City, Washington DC, Philadelphia, and Valley Forge. In July of 2003, we returned to New Jersey. With my brother Jeff and his wife, Kristin, we went to a Baltimore Orioles baseball game and stayed a week by the shore in Cape May, New Jersey. We stayed at the home of my cousin, Walt Wright. We were with Jeff and Kristin, as well as my sister Elin, her husband, Clint, their daughter, Becky, and Becky's friend.

In September of 2003, we went to Houston to visit Elin and Clint and then to San Antonio to visit Sharon's son, Randy and his family. We went to NASA and to a Texas Rangers baseball game. In San Antonio, we saw the River Walk, Japanese Gardens, and the Alamo.

In March of 2004, we traveled to San Francisco to visit friends and to celebrate our first anniversary.

In May of 2004, we went to Florida and saw Disney World. We

traveled up the East Coast to St. Augustine, Savannah, and Tybee Island in Georgia, and Charleston, South Carolina.

In March of 2005, we spent a few days in New York City with my cousin and his wife, Walt and Leslie Wright. We went to a couple of Broadway plays, museums, and the United Nations, where Leslie volunteers.

In May of 2005, we went to Disneyland in California. During that same month we went to Zion and Bryce National Parks with our friends Dolores and Bill Morro. In July 2006, we traveled with Jeff and Kristin through Yellowstone Park and to Jackson Hole, Wyoming. In September of 2006, we again went to the East Coast and saw Williamsburg, Jamestown, and Yorktown, Virginia. In December of 2006, we went to Las Vegas to see BYU play football in a bowl game. They played Oregon and won! We stayed at the New York New York Hotel and also saw the Blue Men perform.

In August of 2007, we went to San Francisco with Sharon's daughter Kassie, her husband, James, and their son, Daxton. During the same month, Sharon and I went through Yellowstone National Park on our way to Billings to see Elin and Clint. In May of 2008, Sharon and I went to Florida. We spent a couple of days in Miami, and then we drove up to Orlando to Walt Disney World. We saw The Magic Kingdom, Animal Park, Epcot, and MGM Studios all in three days. We drove back to Miami to board a cruise ship to the Caribbean. In July of 2008, Sharon and I went to Bear Lake, Utah, for a family reunion with all of my kids and grandkids. While at Bear Lake, we fished, swam, went to Ice Caves, and saw a couple of plays. It was a lot of fun.

It has been just awesome to live so close to Brigham Young University. We belong to the Cougar Club and have season tickets to all of the football and basketball games. It is probably what we both love the most, attending the games, especially when they win.

They have incredibly talented students at BYU, and we attend a lot of the plays, musicals, vocal groups, and dance productions.

CHAPTER NINETEEN

Memories—National Wrestling Hall of Fame

—A Good Life

My Children

I've always felt lucky to have good children who are quite athletic by nature.

All five have graduated from college and are self-sufficient. They have all chosen good spouses, also college graduates, and all live in good homes.

Cheryl is the oldest daughter. When she was in junior high school in 1979, she tried out for song girl and was cut from the squad. She again tried out for song girl when she was a freshman in high school, and was again cut from the squad. She was discouraged and talked to her mother, who told her she should keep trying, that she could make it. Cheryl tried again for song girl her sophomore year and was accepted. After that, she won several speech and dance contests and she became the senior song girl.

When she was a junior, she told the people in charge that she thought it was wrong to have to buy new song girl outfits every year, since it was very expensive for parents. The leaders listened to her and changed their policy; as a result, many parents saved a great deal of money. Cheryl won a scholarship and graduated from Brigham Young University.

Today Cheryl is married to Kent Cummings, and they have six children. She is a senior probation officer for the Alpine School District. Kent works for the Department of Natural Resources as a park ranger and supervisor.

Jimmy, my second child and first son, has always been an outstanding athlete and was a star in baseball at Brigham Young University-Hawaii. Jimmy received his master's degree from Columbia University in Organizational Behavior and currently works as a recruiter for Prince Perelson and Associates in Salt Lake City. It is hard to believe that he makes twice as much as I made as a special agent in the FBI. Jimmy is married to Heather, and they have two daughters.

My third child, Brian, has always given 100 percent to everything he has attempted. Brian served a mission for The Church of Jesus Christ of Latter-day Saints in Bahia Blanca, Argentina, from December of 1991 through December of 1993. Brian graduated from Weber State University in Utah with a major in criminal justice. While employed as a police officer in Murray, Utah, Brian was called up to serve with the National Guard in Iraq. When his commanding officer, Staff Sergeant Cowley, was killed, Brian became the troop leader. During this time, his troops were involved in several gun battles. When Brian returned to the United States, he received several medals at Fort Douglas in Salt Lake City. All of the soldiers who fought with him in Iraq were at the ceremony. After he received his medals, his troops came up to him, and each one of them gave him a bear hug. I have never seen anything like that in my life.

Brian was also honored by the Murray City Council and is employed by Murray City as a detective in the police department. Brian is married to Lindsey, and they have three children.

Jerry is the fourth child. When Jerry was in junior high, our family was living in San Ramon. Our house faced a row of houses on the other side of the street and above those houses was a large hill with deer and occasionally even a fox. Each day Jerry would go out and then come back inside and tell his mother what he saw. One day our neighbor, a newlywed named Becky Bronson, was in her front yard when Jerry ran outside, jumped off the porch, waved to the deer and yelled, "Hello, deer." Becky waved back at Jerry and said, "Hello, Jerry." When Jerry went back inside the house, his face was bright red. His mother asked what was wrong and Jerry told her their next-door neighbor thought that he had just called her "dear."

Jerry became an Eagle Scout and served a mission for The Church of Jesus Christ of Latter-day Saints in Lisbon, Portugal, from November 1994 through November 1996. Jerry received a degree in accounting from Utah State University and also received his master's degree in business from Utah State in 2004. He is now a CPA. Jerry works as an executive vice president for JD Clark and Company in Ogden, Utah. Jerry is married to Sally, and they have three children. Sally is a newspaper columnist.

My fifth child, Kimberly, is a sweet, kind person who always tries to do what is right. It is amazing how much she is like her mother, Karen. She was always very close to her mother and emulates her in many ways. Kim graduated from the Utah Valley University in Orem in Behavioral Science with an emphasis in psychology. Kim is married to Daniel Stovall, and they have two children. They named their little girl Karen, after Kim's mother. Daniel is a senior software engineer for Parlant Technology.

I have had a lot of fun with my family. Every year our family went on a vacation, and we've shared some wonderful memories. We've been to Disneyland, Knott's Berry Farm, Universal Studios. Muir Woods, various camping sites, Cape May, New Jersey, Beavercreek, Ohio, Billings and Red Lodge, Montana, Philadelphia, Yellowstone Park, various family reunions, South Lake Tahoe, Hearst Castle, Amish country in Intercourse, Pennsylvania, water rafting, and the San Diego Zoo. We used to travel to Yellowstone Park and see over a hundred bears. Most of the bears have now been taken out of Yellowstone and it is hard to see any today.

The Wright families started having reunions in Cape May, New Jersey, in the summer of 1990. Since then, the families have had a reunion in Cape May every five years. At each family reunion, all the members are given T-shirts. The T-shirts would say things such as, "It is hard to be wrong when you are Wright," or "The Wright Stuff," or "The Wright Time – The Wright Place." The last reunion was held in the summer of 2005. It is fun to see 135 of your relatives at the beach in Cape May walking around wearing the same T-shirts.

In July of 2000, I was able to go to Calgary, Canada, with my sister Elin and her husband Clint, who is from Canada, and two of their children, Meagan and Becky. It was an absolutely wonderful trip, and we saw beautiful sights. We camped in Banff and saw the Sulfur Mountains, Lake Louise, and the Columbia ice fields. We watched the Calgary Stampede, which was very exciting.

In October of 2002, I went back to Woodbury to help my brother get his house ready to sell. We spent three weeks painting and fixing up the house and then my brother Jeff and I went to Intercourse, Pennsylvania, to see the Amish. We sold the house, loaded up a huge truck, and drove with two other men across the country to Utah, where Jeff moved with his wife, Kristin.

In November of 2002, my brothers Jeff, Dave, and I went on a trip in Dave's boat, the Voyager IV. We traveled from Bear, Delaware, to Florida and had a great time on the trip. Dave paid for all of our expenses. I will always remember all of the things I saw while aboard that boat.

A lifetime of sports and various assignments by the FBI have left me with indelible memories. If not for a wrestling career that started at Woodbury High School, I would not have had either.

Hall of Fame Awards

Sports have always been a big part of my life and I continued playing softball, racquetball, and golf into my sixties. On November 6, 2004, I was inducted into the South Jersey Wrestling Hall of Fame. On March 22, 2005, I was inducted into the Gloucester County New Jersey Sports Hall of Fame. On September 24, 2006, I was inducted into the National Wrestling Hall of Fame as an Outstanding American. Two of the previous inductees into the National Wrestling Hall of Fame at the time were a U.S. Supreme Court justice and Secretary of Defense Donald Rumsfeld.

The first newspaper article was published in the *Gloucester County Times* in Woodbury, New Jersey, and is dated November 7, 2004. The article reads as follows:

Herd Grad Owes FBI Career to Wrestling
By Bill Evans

James Wright chased Patty Hearst across California, interviewed followers of cult figure Jim Jones, spent countless hours examining evidence trying to capture the Unabomber and made a career apprehending bank robbers.

He owes it all to wrestling at Woodbury High School. Wright, who was inducted into the South Jersey Wrestling Hall of Fame Saturday night, parlayed his wrestling ability at Woodbury into a scholarship at Brigham Young. Though he completed only one year before suffering a career-ending knee injury, he earned his degree and went on to become a high school teacher and coach, eventually returning to his alma mater where he was head wrestling coach for two years and convinced eventual state champion Howard Pendleton to come out for the team.

In 1970, Wright took the advice of his secretary and applied for the Federal Bureau of Investigation. He was hired and became one of the FBI's top agents for over a quarter-century.

"My secretary at Woodbury was Pat Carter, and her husband was an agent," said Wright, who retired in 1997 but still works for the agency part-time. "They were hiring 1,000 agents because there was a rash of hijackings and she thought I would be a good agent. I really liked teaching and coaching, so I was a little skeptical but she said if I write your letter, will you sign it? I was hired, immediately doubled my salary, and it kept skyrocketing."

Wright didn't plan to attend college as he didn't think he could afford it, but Woodbury wrestling coach, Bill Morro was able to find his charge a scholarship after Wright won a region title and wrestled in the 106-pound state final his senior year in 1962.

"He came up to me and said, 'I can get you a scholarship. Where do you want to go?'" recalled Wright, who now lives in Utah. "I had some friends out at BYU so I said BYU. Within a couple of days, he got me a scholarship to BYU.

"He cared about what you did. If I wouldn't have gone to college, forget about getting into the Bureau. I got an opportunity and I'm glad I had it. Bill cared about all his athletes, and I owe it all to him."

To Morro, Wright was an amazing athlete who could succeed at whatever he tried and just needed a chance to exploit his abilities.

"I first met him in the seventh grade when he was playing sandlot ball on the playgrounds in the city," said Morro. "He was about 90 pounds, but he had good hands and all the talent. When he came here, he wrestled but he also ran cross-country and played tennis, and he was good at all three. He'd have been a great shortstop or even a guard in basketball. He always worked hard. To me, he was just a natural. I'll tell you, he's one guy who would never call it quits. He was a hard worker and put that together with his ability, you couldn't ask for anybody better. I knew sooner or later some (Hall of Fame) would recognize him. He has a great resume."

Once in the FBI, Wright worked his way up to being one of the top agents, spending 23 years in San Francisco. Among his more high-profile cases were the Patty Hearst kidnapping (1974-75); the Chowchilla, California, kidnapping of a busload of school children (1976); the Rev. Jim Jones' Peoples' Temple mass suicide of 913 members (1978); the Walker/Whitworth espionage case where classified information was sold to the Soviet Union (1986); the Freeman Montana case (1996); and the Theodore Kaczynski Unabomber case (1996).

Wright spent a good portion of his career working bank robberies by choice, though he also spent a period focusing on foreign counterintelligence.

"Generally, most bank robbers had a tough life," said Wright. "Some of the stories would rip you apart. I never had a bank robber get less than 12 years. We caught one guy who thought his partner was holding out on him, which he wasn't, and the guy shot him in the head and threw him off a cliff. Did I get some dangerous people off the street? Yeah, I did. Am I proud of it? Yes, I am. When I retired

I requested my file with the Freedom of Information Act, and there wasn't one negative thing in there."

During his FBI career, Wright still found time to stay active in athletics, playing softball into the 1980s and winning tournaments in ping pong and tennis. He also coached high school sports in California.

"I've got trophies coming out my ears," said Wright. "I stayed heavily involved with sports, but I'm 61 now, so I'm not sliding into bases any more."

Wright is not apprehending bank robbers any more either, but a lifetime of sports and FBI work has left indelible memories. If not for a wrestling career that started at Woodbury High School, he might not have had either.

"Jimmy's always said that he owes his career to me, and if that's the way he feels there's not much else I could say about it," said Morro. "It's all part of the job for me. Building special friendships like I have with him is part of the deal too. It's outstanding what he's been able to do. He's had a heck of a career."

JIM AND SHARON AT THE SOUTH JERSEY
WRESTLING HALL OF FAME

The *Gloucester County Times* published another article on August 17, 2006, which reads as follows:

Former Woodbury Wrestler to Join National Hall of Fame
By The Times Sports Staff

Jim Wright, a former Woodbury High School wrestler who enjoyed an illustrious career with the FBI, and Art Marinelli, a former two-time state champion who founded the wrestling program at Oakcrest High School, are among the seven inductees into the New Jersey Chapter of the National Wrestling Hall of Fame in September.

Wright is being honored as an Outstanding American. He has devoted his professional life to help preserve the peace and safety of our country, serving for 26 years as a distinguished member of the Federal Bureau of Investigation. During his work at the FBI, Wright earned 25 letters of commendation for excellence in the fulfillment of his responsibilities.

In fact, one of the letters of commendation is from the President of the United States. Commendation for cases involved extortion, illegal drugs, bombings, bank robberies, espionage and foreign counter intelligence, terrorism, kidnapping, murder, organized crime, theft of interstate shipments and mail fraud.

Wright has an exceptional record of accomplishment in dealing with many high profile cases, including the Patty Hearst kidnapping, the Chowchilla California kidnapping of a bus load of school children, the Reverend Jim Jones mass suicide, the Walker/Whitworth espionage case in which classified information was sold to the Soviet Union, the search and capture of Theodore Kaczynski, the Unabomber, and the kidnapping of an hours-old baby from a Canadian hospital.

Wright also devoted much of his time to the capture of bank robbers. He was so successful in this effort that the California Savings and Loan Association in the San Francisco Bay area honored him with a special award for arresting 15 bank robbers in one year.

Much of Wright's success in life he credits to his involvement at Woodbury High School in the sport of wrestling and to Coach Bill Morro. When Wright was a seventh grade student at Woodbury, he met Morro, who encouraged him to try wrestling, and thus began a lifelong relationship with his coach and friend.

Wright had exceptional athletic ability and the self-discipline and desire to succeed. He earned seven varsity letters in three sports: wrestling, cross-country, and tennis. In wrestling he won a regional title and placed second in the State Tournament.

On scholarship to Brigham Young University, he wrestled varsity for two years, winning all of his matches his freshman year except one and earning a third-place finish in the Western Athletic Conference. A knee injury sidelined him and halted a promising college career.

Wright epitomizes the qualities of leadership on which American society depends: honesty, commitment, self-discipline, self-reliance and confidence—qualities he learned through his participation in the sport of wrestling.

JIM BEING HONORED WITH A JACKET AND PLAQUE AT THE
NATIONAL WRESTLING HALL OF FAME

I have enjoyed writing this book and remembering details of the cases I have worked over the years. I hope the readers have enjoyed it as well. It was fun working for the FBI, and they have always treated me fairly. I never thought I would be an agent. It really is amazing the things a person can accomplish if he or she is willing to work hard.

I retired as a special agent with the FBI in January of 1997. Since retiring, I have worked as a special investigator for the Bureau, but full retirement is just around the corner. With our combined families, Sharon and I have nine children and twenty-two grandchildren. We certainly keep busy with family, church, BYU sports (as spectators), and traveling. I am very content with life and will continue to enjoy the coming years.

CPSIA information can be obtained at www.ICGtesting.com
Printed in the USA
BVOW04s1953200514

354054BV00009B/51/P